RUMO IS CALLING

Glenda Bacca

LUMINARE PRESS
WWW.LUMINAREPRESS.COM

Rumo Is Calling
Copyright © 2020 by Glenda Bacca

All rights reserved. This book or any portion thereof may not be reproduced or used in any manner whatsoever without the express written permission of the publisher, except for the use of brief quotations in a book review.

Printed in the United States of America

Cover Design by Melissa K. Thomas

Luminare Press
442 Charnelton St.
Eugene, OR 97401
www.luminarepress.com

LCCN: 2020905659
ISBN: 978-1-64388-340-3

This book is dedicated to all of my family, American and Italian. The branches on our family tree span many directions, but we are bound by deep roots. The essence of who we are is passed down from generation to generation. I am grateful for my family, the history we share, and the love that binds us together.

Of course, what would life be without those special friends who support us, love us unconditionally, and make us laugh. You know who you are! Thank you for being a part of my life.

Giorgio (Claudio) Paris – Angela Graziella Dardanello
1952   1949

Andrea Paris – 1978
Erica Paris – 1980

Luigi Leonardi – Luciana Fox
1944   1941–2018

Ilaria Leonardi – 1971
Elisa Leonardi – 1973
Anna Leonardi –1978

Bruno Paris – Mariagrazia Vender
1946   1959

Romina Paris – 1986
Roberta Paris – 1993

Lucia Leonardi – Renzo Demagri
1941   1936

Paola Demagri – 1965
Fabio Demagri – 1967
Franco Demagri –1967

Natalia Bacca – Vittorio Paris
1908–2000   1892–1968

Bruno Paris – 1946
Giorgio Paris – 1952

Rosa Bacca – Igino Leonardi
1907–1981   1902–1980

Lucia Leonardi – 1941
Giovanni Leonardi – 1942
Luigi Leonardi –1944

Carlo Fanti – Lucia Bevilacqua
1929   1938–1982

Alessandra Fanti – 1964
Milva Fanti – 1965

Giovanni Bacca – Maria Eccher
1869–1922   1877–1948

Angela Bacca – 1901–1991
Olivia Bacca – 1903–1980
Catterina Bacca –1905–2004
Rosa Bacca – 1907–1981
Natalia Bacca – 1908–2000
Adele Bacca – 1910–1977
Giovanni Bacca – 1912–1990
Giuseppe Bacca – 1913–1991
Ida Bacca – 1915–2013
Livio Bacca – 1921–2001

Angela Bacca – Alessandro Fanti
1901–1991   1888–1964

Olga Fanti – 1924–1975
Bice Fanti – 1926–2012
Carlo Fanti –1929

Olga Fanti – Vittorio Paris
1924–1975   1920–1958

Luciano Paris – 1950
Vinicio Paris – 1952
Alessandro Paris – 1957-1988

Bice Fanti – Celestino Fanti
1926–2012   1920–1986

Roberto Fanti – 1954
Ugo Fanti – 1955
Vittorio Fanti – 1958

Ugo Fanti – Loredana Vinante
1955   1964

Marinella Fanti – 1993
Gabriele Fanti – 1995

Giovanni Bacca – Cattarina Martinelli
1826–1879   1842

Dominica Bacca – 1865
Maria Bacca – 1867–1939
Giovanni Bacca – 1869–1922
Vigilio Bacca – 1871–1942
Alessandro Bacca – 1873–1948
Nicolo Bacca – 1876–1932
Lorenzo Bacca – 1878

Livo Bacca – Elsa Fosser
1921–2001   1925–2012

Giovanni Bacca – 1950
Anita Bacca – 1952
Elio Bacca – 1957
Franca Bacca – 1961

Giovanni Bacca – Rosanna Pellegrini
1950   1953

Cristina Bacca – 1982

Elio Bacca
1957

Ida Bacca – Dante Nardelli
1915–2013   1913–1988

Franco Nardelli – 1948–2016
Sergio Nardelli – 1949
Romeo Nardelli – 1952
Paolo Nardelli – 1957

Anita Bacca – Mario Folgheraiter
1952   1947

Monica Folgheraiter – 1976
Andrea Folgheraiter – 1984

Giuseppe Bacca – Adelfina Marchesi
1913–1991   1923–1988

Lino Bacca – 1946
Enzo Bacca – 1948
Ada Bacca – 1951–2017

Franca Bacca – Franco Lucchini
1961   1959

Nadia Lucchini – 1991
Stefano Lucchini – 1994

Frank Bacca – Annetta Mitchell
1909–1961   1925–2006

Robert Bacca – 1940
Carol Horton (Step-Daughter) – 1947
Rebecca Bacca – 1953–2003
Jo Ann Bacca – 1954
William Bacca – 1955
Glenda Bacca – 1956
James Bacca – 1959

Alexander Bacca – Agnes (Babe) Carbonneau
1907–1990   1906–1999

Alexander P. Bacca – 1938–2013

John Bacca – Anna Coppi
1905–1974   1917–2005

Lucille Bacca – 1938
Katherine Bacca – 1939
Virginia Bacca – 1941

Joseph Bacca – Anna Menapace
1906–1998   1909–1983

Margaret Bacca – 1927
Fred Bacca – 1931–2003
Carolyn Bacca – 1934

Alessandro Bacca – Margherita Aimo
1873–1948   1888–1927

John Bacca – 1905–1974
Joseph Bacca – 1906–1998
Frank Bacca – 1909–1961

Nicolo Bacca – Candida Fanti
1876–1932   1883–1963

Alexander Nicholas Bacca – 1907–1990
Angelina Bacca – 1908–2003
Erma Bacca – 1910–1998

Chapter One

As I begin to stir, I remember going to bed exhausted and am thankful I slept well throughout the night. Although not yet fully awake, I can sense the room is full of light. I am aware of the beautiful church bells in the distance, the music of birds chirping loudly, and somewhere a rooster crowing while hens cluck good morning.

Awakening fully, I realize, *It's not Sunday. Rooster and chickens in Turlock? Oh, my word, this is not Turlock! I'm here. I made it. It is my first full day in Rumo!* Excited, I jump out of bed and rush to the living room windows to gaze upon my new surroundings.

Having arrived in Rumo the night before just as it was getting dark, I could not get a real sense of my new neighborhood. Peering out one window, I am stunned by a gorgeous mountain outside my door. It is mid-April. The trees and grass on the hillside are shades of luscious green. There is a garden below full of colorful tulips; beside it stands two fruit trees in bloom with birds fluttering around full of song. Some distance away, a charming little church sits atop a hill surrounded by apple trees so full of white blossoms the hillside appears to be covered in snow. Taking in this amazing view, I reflect on the trip here as well as my evening last night with my new landlord and his family.

When I was getting ready to retire from thirty-four years in education, several people wanted to know what I was going to do with my time. I responded, "I'm going to Italy to find my family!" I retired at the end of August, finding the courage to move forward by mid-October. I searched the internet for places to rent in Corte Superiore, Italy. After scanning the options, I found a nice apartment for a price I could afford.

I wanted an extended stay because it might take some time to search church records, other city records, and to talk to people to see if I could determine if family lived in the area. I sent a request to rent this apartment for six months, receiving an immediate response that it was available, and the price would be reduced for such an extended stay. I had twenty-four hours to accept this new price offer.

Suddenly, I got cold feet. I had never traveled outside the United States on my own. I didn't read or speak Italian. I didn't know a single person in Italy. *I must be crazy to do this!* When I did not reply to the offer, I received a nice email from a man named Giorgio.

"Hello, Glenda. I did not hear back from you. Are you still interested in my apartment? Was there a problem with the offer? Is there something I can do to assist you?"

"Hello, Giorgio. My name is Glenda Bacca, and I recently retired. Now that I have time, I want to come to Italy to find my family. My grandfather was born in Corte Superiore. I realized after I sent my request to rent your apartment, I first need to find someone who has time to help me search for family in addition to translating for me. I also need to verify that I can stay in Italy for six full months with nothing but a passport."

Giorgio replied, "I, too, am retired. I worked for the municipality for many years, and part of my job was to help people find family. I will help you. Come to Italy! If this is your first visit to our area, I will also be your tour guide. There are many wonderful things to see here. Come to Italy! I checked with my friend at the municipality. You can only stay three months on a passport. If you want to tell me your grandfather's name, when he was born, and the name of his parents, I will start searching for you now."

I was hesitant to share this information because I wanted to learn myself about my family but decided it would not hurt. "Thank you for your generous offer," I replied. "My grandfather was Alessandro Bacca. I believe his father was Giovanni and his mother Cattarina Martinelli." We agreed I would come for three months and finalized the dates for my stay with my arrival set for mid-April in Verona, where Giorgio would meet me at the airport.

My next email exchange with Giorgio occurred on Christmas Eve. "Merry Christmas, Glenda. I thought it would be a good time to send you the photo attached. It is a photo of the house your grandfather was born in. I hope you like this gift. Also, I will tell you there are two Baccas living in this house. I have not told them you are coming to Italy. I want to surprise them. I have other surprises for you, but I cannot tell all now. I want to surprise you when you arrive in April. Merry Christmas—Giorgio, Wanda, and Sandro." *Who are Wanda and Sandro? They must be Giorgio's family.*

The photo depicted a large, almost octagonal house, with numerous shuttered windows, and an arched garage door. Overwhelmed with joy, I immediately emailed my family to share the photo from Giorgio. His news heightened my excitement. I went shopping, buying far more clothes than I could possibly need. I packed two suitcases one month before my departure date. I could not wait for April to get here!

A few days before departing, I emailed Giorgio to ask about the weather, suddenly concerned that I was not taking enough warm clothes. It was already warm in Turlock. Typical temperatures would be well into the nineties in May and into the hundreds in June. Realizing that I was going to Northern Italy in the Alps, I wondered if perhaps my choice in clothing needed to be altered. After a couple of email exchanges, Giorgio realized I had misunderstood him. He clarified that it would in fact be cool when I arrived and to bring a few warm clothes.

The next day, I received a message from Vito, Giorgio's brother. He had lived in Canada for forty years so naturally spoke English. Vito shared that he had recently spoken with his brother. Giorgio was concerned that he did not know English well, limiting his ability to communicate with me. Vito offered his services. Should I have questions or need help, I was free to message him anytime for clarification.

How absolutely thoughtful of both Giorgio and Vito, I thought. Without even having met me, they want to ensure that I am able to communicate in Italy. Through emails alone, I have already established a friendship with Giorgio. I am certain he is a man I can trust.

My flight arrived on time, but my luggage did not. Not the best way to start my trip. Exiting the arrival area, I scanned the lobby. I spotted a handsome, elderly gentleman standing there with a photo of my grandfather's house with the words "Welcome Home Glenda" written on it in big red letters. *What a delightful way to be greeted.* We also greeted each other with the typical Italian kiss on each cheek. As we drove from Verona to Rumo, I was nervous and anxious. Fatigue, lost luggage, being in a strange environment, and not being the best conversationalist all added to my anxiety. Not long into the drive, Giorgio put me at ease with his banter. We chatted about many things.

"When I reported my luggage missing, I gave them your name and number to call when they find it. Is that OK?"

"Certo, Glenda. It is no problem. I will call them tomorrow to check. You flew from Rome to Verona?"

"No, I came from Paris to Verona. Paris is a huge airport. I could not believe how big. My layover was four hours. I am surprised my luggage did not make it on the plane."

"Oh, that happens often, but they will find it and deliver it to Rumo. Don't worry. Tell me about the town where you live."

"Turlock is a large city, about eighty thousand people. When I first moved to Turlock it was fifteen thousand people, so it has grown over the years. It is in the center of California in an area called the San Joaquin Valley. It is an agricultural area."

"Really, what do you grow in Turlock?"

"Over the years many things have been grown near Turlock, but now mostly peaches, walnuts, almonds, and grapes. My brother who owns an almond farm lives in a town nearby. Also, in this town is a large cheese factory. In another town nearby is a large winery."

"So, you are not in the mountains? What is it like in Turlock?"

"It is very hot in Turlock in the summer with many days over a hundred degrees. Turlock is in a terrific location though, because in a two-to-three-hour drive you arrive at many interesting places: San Francisco, Napa Valley, Yosemite National Park, Lake Tahoe, Monterey, Sacramento. When it gets too hot, you can get out of Turlock; it is easy to go to cooler areas."

"Oh, Yosemite. I have always wanted to go to Yosemite. It is my dream to be there."

"Yes, Yosemite is beautiful and very popular for tourists. If you come to California one day, I will take you to Yosemite. Tell me about Rumo. I know it is in the Trentino–Alto Adige region, but I don't know much else about it."

"Yes, the region is divided into two provinces. Rumo is in the Trentino province. Trento is the largest city of about one hundred thousand people. There are many valleys in the mountains, with Rumo being in Val di Non. Rumo is a commune—a small community—made up of six small villages. Corte Superiore where your grandfather was born is one village. The apartment you will live in is in Mione. I live in Mocenigo. The other villages are Marcena, Lanza, and Corte Inferiore."

"How many people live in Rumo?"

"Once there were about fifteen hundred people in Rumo, but now there are only seven to eight hundred people. There is not enough work in our area, so the young people have to leave to go find work."

"I see many grapevines. Are there a lot of wineries here?"

"Of course. Wine is very important in Italy. We, too, have a big winery near us, but in our valley, we are known for our apples. The Trentino region produces almost 60 percent of the apples grown in Italy."

While we drove, I looked out on the scenery: hills and mountains everywhere, filled with green trees, vineyards, and apple orchards. The towns were a mix of extremely old buildings along with newer construction. The highway was two lanes on both sides; however, as we got off the highway, we were on a one lane road. At one point Giorgio asked me, "Are you going to rent a car, Glenda?"

"I was not planning on it. I read that there are buses from Rumo that will take you to various towns where you can catch the train. Therefore, I planned to use the bus and train to get around."

"Oh, Glenda, I do not think you understand how separated Rumo is from other places. The buses and trains are not reliable in Italy. They often do not run on time. I do not want you to get stranded. Maybe I cannot always be available to come find you. You need to rent a car. We will go rent one tomorrow."

My anxiety doubled. I had never driven in a foreign country. I had not studied anything on the driving laws or road signs in Italy. However, I must have anticipated this as I had gotten an international driver's license just in case. *The expense of renting a car for three months will be extreme. I did not plan on it. Thank God for credit cards.*

We stopped in a small town at a bar for a glass of white wine to celebrate my arrival. *How did Giorgio know that I love wine?* As we arrived in Rumo, there was a sign that read "Benvenuti a Rumo." I shouted, "We're here, Giorgio. We are in Rumo!"

He chuckled, "Yes, this first village is Marcena. It is the biggest village in Rumo. It has the bank, post office, and municipal office. We are going first to my house where my wife, Wanda, is fixing us a little dinner. I have invited my friend Daniel to come. He speaks English and will help to communicate if needed."

Poor Giorgio, I thought. He must really be worried about

his English. First his brother contacts me. Now his friend who speaks English is coming to dinner. He is worrying too much. So far, I have understood him fine.

Giorgio turned left onto another road. Shortly after turning, I saw a sign, "Corte Superiore." In my excitement, I flung my arm out, hitting Giorgio in the arm as I shouted, "Corte Superiore! Is this it? Is this where my grandfather was born?"

"Calma, Glenda, calma. Keep calm. OK, I will take you." As Giorgio turned right on a road, in front of my eyes was the house my grandfather was born in. I recognized it immediately from the photo Giorgio had sent me. Emotion filled me to the point I could not speak. "We cannot go in Glenda," he said. "I have not made arrangements with your family yet, and Wanda is waiting for us with dinner. You will see it one day." I could hardly wait!

At Giorgio's house I met Wanda; Sandro, his son; and Daniel, his friend. Upon meeting Wanda, she asked me in Italian, "Woman to woman, how old are you?"

I laughed, replying in my very limited Italian, "I am fifty-eight years old."

"Only fifty-eight. You are young to be retired."

I smiled as I nodded my head. They invited me to have a seat at the table. Giorgio poured us wine. On the table was antipasto of bread, cheese, prosciutto, and pancetta. Soon Wanda served us the first course, a bowl of delicious rice soup. Daniel and Giorgio interpreted as we conversed.

Daniel asked, "What work did you do?"

I tried to think of the words to respond in Italian, but it was too difficult. "I worked in the public schools," I responded, "at first working as a speech-language pathologist. I worked with children who had handicaps and needed assistance in learning to talk. When I began working, I helped children who were deaf or hard of hearing, then later children who had Down syndrome, autism, and other disabilities. After about fifteen years, I went into administration, helping to run programs for children with disabilities. The last five years I was the director, the big boss who oversaw all of the programs for children with disabilities in a school district. I don't think it was the best job for me. I found it too stressful. After five years, I decided to retire."

Giorgio responded, "Brava. You are a good woman to work with children who have problems like this. It is not easy work. You must have a kind heart."

"Thank you. Sometimes I wish I had not gone into administration, that I had continued to work directly with the children, yet overall it was a fine career."

"Tell us about your family. Do you have brothers or sisters? Why did it take you so long to come to Rumo to find family?"

"Well, I don't know how much you want to know, but I was born in the small town of Raton, New Mexico, population approximately ten thousand people. I am from a large family, seven children: four girls and three boys. I am sixth in line. My father was born in Dawson, New Mexico, a small mining town that no longer exists."

Daniel interjected, "Many Italians left Italy to go work in the mines in America. There were big advertisements about working in the mines. People here were extremely poor and needed work."

"Yes, there were many Italians in Dawson; sadly, many were killed from two different mine explosions. Everything, including the buildings, was owned by the mining company, so when the mine closed in 1950, the entire town was dismantled and residents moved elsewhere. My family moved to the nearby town of Raton. My father was a first-generation American, his father having immigrated in the late 1800s. I did not know my Italian grandparents, as they both died before I was born. My father had died when I was five years old; therefore, he was not around to tell me stories of his life or of family."

Sandro asked, "So how did you learn you had family here in Rumo?"

"I became interested in finding information about my grandfather's family around 1970, when I was about thirteen. There was no internet at the time; therefore, you could not easily search for people. My father had two brothers, each with three children. When I talked with them, they could not remember much about my grandfather's family, and I received conflicting information from the two families. They told me he was from Tyrol, Italy."

They all laughed. Giorgio interjected, "That is not a town. That is a large area that belonged to Austria but now includes Austria in addition to Italy."

"Yes, I learned that when I tried to find Tyrol in the encyclopedia. When the internet became available in the 1990s, I searched online, finding references to other Baccas, but I could not be positive that they were related to my grandfather.

"After one of my uncles died in 1998, his daughter gave me a small brown suitcase that she had found at his house. This suitcase was full of treasures. It had business documents, receipts showing taxes paid, and receipts documenting money he sent to family in Italy. It also had a map of Italy with a circle in yellow that highlighted Rumo, Marcena, and Mocenigo. The greatest treasures were letters written to my grandfather from his family in Italy. The return address on the letters was Corte Superiore, Italy. I did not understand the connection between the towns on the map and Corte Superiore, but at long last, I had references to towns plus some names of relatives.

"By the time I had this information, I was rather busy at work, preventing me from taking a significant amount of time to search for family. When I was younger, I was also afraid to travel outside of the United States by myself. I have been to Italy three times before but always on a tour with groups of people supported by tour guides to help me. Given that I am older, coupled with technology, I decided I could be brave and come alone."

I continued to answer questions as we chatted. They could see that I was getting very tired after such a long trip. I said goodbye to Wanda and Sandro. Giorgio and Daniel took me to my new apartment where I would live for the next few months. Daniel graciously gave me his telephone number, encouraging me to call if I need anything.

Chapter Two

After taking in the beauty outside my apartment, I realized today will be a challenge. With no suitcases, I have limited clothing options, no curling iron, no contact lenses, and no makeup. I feel disheveled and out of sorts. I had studied Italian through a computer program, but I am concerned that I will not be able to communicate. Limited skills or not, I have to go to the grocery store to get food. It is Saturday; I know the store will be closed tomorrow. Giorgio had told me where the store is located, so I venture out. Walking to the store, I familiarize myself with my new neighborhood.

Stepping out of my apartment, I immediately smell the perfume emanating from the huge lilac bush in full bloom just outside my door. *Gorgeous, absolutely gorgeous.* There is a very narrow road to the right. *Where does that road go? Maybe later I will go exploring to see what is at the end of that road.* Directly in front of me is an old, small building that appears to be a shed or storage facility. There is no house next to it, which makes me wonder who it belongs to. Beyond the shed, to my left, there are homes. All of the buildings are two or three stories tall. It is evident that some of them have garages as the first floor. The buildings are well maintained; some appear newer than others. My apartment seems to be in a cluster at the end of a street down the hill from the main road.

Walking toward the main road, I go between two buildings that are exceptionally close together. *How did Giorgio's car manage to make it through this space? It is so narrow.* Next, I come to an old church, built in the 1500s. *Why do I not remember driving past this church last night? The church bells I heard this morning seemed further away. I need to visit this church later.* I am certain I am going in the correct direction when I come to the hill. We had driven down a very steep hill last night from the main road. *Wow, I am going to get my exercise going up this hill every day.* The view from this hill, as I climb, is stunning. Stopping to look out at the valley, I am awed by the blue sky, soft white clouds, rolling hills of green, small towns in the distance, and tall snow-capped mountains.

When I arrive at the store, there is a sign on the door that says they are closed for a special event. Giorgio and Wanda had kindly left me apples, cookies, orange juice, and coffee in the apartment, but that would not be enough to sustain me for two days. Walking back to the apartment, I notice a bar, Bar Lanterna. The bars in Italy are not merely places to consume alcohol but also serve as restaurants in addition to places for social gatherings. As I enter the bar, anxiety and fear fill me. I cannot think of a single word in Italian.

The woman behind the bar looks at me, smiling broadly. She says something, and I respond with a puzzled expression. Suddenly seeing bags of chips, I point to them. She hands me a bag, saying something else I do not understand. Then she asks, "Panino?" *Oh, sandwich.* I nod yes. "Prosciutto, formaggio?" I nod again, thinking, *of course, ham and cheese.* I manage to say "Grazie" when she gives me my food. Not the best first encounter with the people of Rumo. At least I will not starve!

As I sit eating my small meal, I take in the quaintness of the bar. I watch people come and go, often finding a drink sitting on the counter as they walk up. Obviously, the bartender knows her clients well. She is very attractive and cheerfully greets everyone who comes in. I think I will enjoy coming here in the mornings for a cappuccino. The remainder of the day, I go for a walk along the main road, followed by reading and watching Italian TV programs to practice my Italian.

Sunday, Giorgio and Wanda invite me to join them, along with a group of friends, for pizza dinner. We go to the local pizzeria, Vecchia Segheria. As we sit down at the table, Giorgio asks, "Would you like a *spritzone*?"

"A what? What is that?"

"It is an aperitivo, a before dinner drink. It is common here. We make it special in Trentino. It is made with prosecco wine, Aperol, sparkling water, ice, and a slice of orange. I will order you one. You will like it."

As their friends arrive, I am embarrassed that I do not look my best. I meet three couples: Roland and Elfriede, Ivano and Luisa, and Alessio and Liliana. Thankfully, I have Giorgio to interpret for me, as I am afraid of speaking to a group of people. Their friends seem very accepting of me, trying to include me in conversation. I learn that these are Giorgio and Wanda's best friends. They go hiking together, celebrate together, and rely on each other for support. Giorgio is right. I really like the spritzone. Such an enjoyable evening.

Things improve some after the first weekend. On Monday, I navigate the grocery store without any major incident. Although small and with limited selections, the grocery store has everything you could need. My bags are due to arrive in Trento in the late afternoon. Giorgio plans to take me to get them; in the meantime, he has a niece who works as a travel agent. We visit her, and she is able to get me a tremendous deal on a rental car.

I get a Fiat 500L that is brand new. The car is a stick shift, which I have not driven in a few years. I follow Giorgio home, paying close attention to the road signs so I don't get lost later going out on my own. As I near my new home, it dawns on me, *I have to go down that hill to get to my house. It is only big enough for one car. What do I do if someone else is coming up while I am going down? Then I have to go on that narrow street between the two buildings where there is barely enough space for a car. Can I do it?* I feel relief when I get home and park the car; it will be a while before I get the courage to drive again.

I develop a routine. Every morning, I go to the bar and order a cappuccino and pastry. I learn the woman who owns the bar is Donatella. She always greets me when I come in. We develop a system of communication with her using a few English words and my limited Italian vocabulary, together with gestures. I usually sit outside on the patio at a table where I can enjoy the same breathtaking view of the valley that I have each morning as I walk up the hill. After my coffee, I go for a walk. In the beginning, my daily walks extend from one end of Rumo to the other along the main road. Gradually, I begin to explore different paths.

I am surprised, as I become familiar with the town, how much is here for such a small community. There is not only the post office, municipal office, and bank that Giorgio had pointed out the first day. Rumo also has a carabinieri office, library, theater for performances, doctor's office, pharmacy, tourist office, gas station, hair salon, two hotels, a butcher shop, and a cheese factory. At the hotels, you can get a sauna, pedicure, manicure, and facial. I love all of the houses with window boxes filled with geraniums or other assorted flowers. Conveniently, every village has in its center a public fountain with fresh water flowing from a tap. I can easily fill my water bottle as my walks become longer and longer.

As my comfort level increases, my limited Italian skills come back to me. I greet villagers, responding to simple statements. I realize that the people speak a dialect that I do not know. When people want to have longer conversations, I say, "Mi dispiace. Parlo un poco Italiano. I'm sorry. I speak a little Italian." Some people try using what English they know mixed with Italian. Others go on talking as though I understand everything they say, adding gestures where they think it might be helpful. Everyone is friendly. I am feeling very welcomed in the community.

When I get the courage to drive my little Fiat again, I study a map I found in the apartment. I say to myself, *OK, where shall I go? Pick any place.* As I scan the outstretched map, I see that Fondo is a short distance away. *How about Fondo? I have heard people mention Fondo. It looks like I can go more than one way. This road appears to go northeast through Lauregno, then drops back down into Fondo. This other road goes south through Revò, then east to Fondo. I am confident that either road will get me there. Let's go north first, then return through Revò.*

Off I go with my heart pounding and my hands shaking. Going down the east side of the mountain is scary. It is a one-lane curvy road. In a couple of spots, the road curves so much I am not able to see if other vehicles are coming. If a big truck or bus is heading my way, there will not be enough room for two vehicles. Praying, I make it safely around each curve. I get to the bottom of the road from Rumo and follow the signs to Lauregno. Soon, I realize I am on another curvy, narrow road that seems to go on forever. The longer I drive, the tighter I grip the steering wheel of the car and, likewise, the more I pray I will get there safely.

At last, I arrive in Fondo; my plan is to go to the town center, park the car, and look around the town. However, I find myself driving in circles, never seeing anything I am certain is public parking. In addition, there are a number of cars on this exceedingly narrow street, intensifying my already nervous state. Following the third trip around the town center, I say to myself, *It's OK. I made it here. I feel comfortable with the stick shift. I read the road signs correctly. I can see the town center another day.*

I head home, but soon it dawns on me that I am going in the wrong direction. Having a relatively strong sense of direction, I do not panic or pull over to look at my map. *Surely, I will see a sign soon that will tell me where I am and how I get home.* I am beginning to have my doubts when, finally, there appears a sign that says "Revò."

As I navigate my way along the road to Revò, I notice a similarity to California. I never realized there would be so many little towns that border each other, one right after the other. Every little town has a clear sign marked "Centro," indicating the town center where every town seems to have its own municipal office, bank, post office, and church.

Relieved when I arrive home, I park the car in front of the apartment. *Well, that is enough driving for at least another week.*

Two weeks go by in a flash. It is nearing the end of April. Giorgio is busy with springtime responsibilities. The smell of freshly mowed grass in the air causes my allergies to go crazy. Everyone is planting vegetable gardens, mowing grass, cutting wood, doing home repairs, and looking after beehives. Giorgio knows that I am here for three months; therefore, in his mind, there is no rush to introduce me to family. Nonetheless, I am getting restless. I want to meet the Baccas living in my grandfather's house. I don't want to be rude by banging on the door. If they don't speak any English, how will I communicate with them? I must be patient—not one of my strongest characteristics.

Spring rains are predicted off and on over the next few days. I am glad Giorgio told me to bring some warmer clothes. Early morning and nighttime temperatures can be pretty cool. On rainy days, a turtleneck combined with a sweatshirt are perfect for staying warm.

One morning, I am surprised to see the view out my window. There are large gray clouds suspended between my apartment and the mountain. It is as if you can open the door to walk right out onto the cloud. It has not started to rain yet, but you can feel the moisture in the air. In the afternoon, it rains intermittently; then the clouds disappear, later to be replaced by fog rolling in to cover the area in a huge white blanket. The rain doesn't deter me from my routine. I put on my raincoat, grab my umbrella, and off I go.

Today is Thursday, April 30, another rainy day. I am sitting inside the bar. I have been here enough that I am beginning to recognize the regular customers. As I sit drinking my cappuccino, a man I have not seen before walks in. He places an order at the bar and sits three tables down from me, picking up a newspaper to read. Using the free Wi-Fi at the bar to read emails, check Facebook, and read some news, I am distracted as my eyes keep looking over at this man. *He is rather good-looking: dark wavy hair with gray scattered throughout and broad shoulders. I wonder if he is related to me.* I glance over at the bar. Donatella smiles, raising an eyebrow as she has seen me looking at the man. Embarrassed, I chuckle as I request another cappuccino.

I remain at the bar for a couple hours waiting for the rain to ease up a bit, when I decide it is time to go. As I approach the counter to pay, Donatella answers the phone. I hear her say, "Yes, this is Donatella Fanti." While on the phone, Donatella rings up my order. I pay her before leaving the bar to go on my walk.

While walking, I ponder, *Hmm, Fanti. Donatella's last name is Fanti. Grandpa Alessandro had a brother who married a Fanti from Rumo. I wonder if Donatella could be her relative.*

The next day is yet another rainy day; consequently, I go inside Bar Lanterna to sit. I brought my laptop that contains pictures of family. The bar has an abundance of customers this morning. As I walk to my preferred table, I notice that the attractive man is here again today. He looks up, grinning as I walk past his table, and nods a warm greeting. I nod back thinking, *Wow, nice smile, and look at those big brown eyes.* As I wait for my breakfast, I open my laptop, pulling up the picture of my grandfather's brother Nicolò and his wife, Candida Fanti.

I wait for the bar to clear of so many customers as I eat slowly, sip my coffee, and busy myself with email. Finally, there is only one man sitting at the counter, the handsome stranger at his table, and Donatella. I walk up to the counter with my laptop. Having practiced my Italian the night before, I ask, "Your name is Fanti? Donatella Fanti?" Donatella nods. I show her the picture. "This is my grandfather's brother and his wife. Her name is Candida Fanti. Is she your family?"

Donatella looks at the picture, takes the laptop, and makes the picture larger; she studies the picture again. "No, not my family. You are searching for family?" I nod yes. "What is your name?"

It hits me. *All this time I have greeted people on my walks, had brief conversations, and yet I have never introduced myself. How rude and stupid of me!*

"My name is Glenda. Glenda Bacca. My grandfather was Alessandro Bacca."

I can see the wheels turning in Donatella's head as she ponders. I see a bit of a gleam in her eye, a hint of recognition of the name.

Donatella walks away, returning with a book. "Many old photos of people from Mione. Maybe you will find family in here. You can take it home to look at it."

I thank her. When I turn to go pack up my things at the table, I notice the handsome stranger watching us. He gives me a slight smile and nods again. At home, I look through the book carefully, reading every name. Finding several Baccas, I mark each page with a piece of paper out of a notebook. I cannot wait to see Giorgio again to ask him about all these people.

A couple of days later, it is still raining. I do my usual routine, do some laundry, clean the apartment, and eat lunch. In the afternoon, I am extremely tired. I grab pillows from my bed to take a nap on the couch. As I am getting up after a two-hour nap, the doorbell rings. It is bound to be Giorgio and Wanda, as they come every few days to check on me. I throw open the door, ready to shout "Buona sera!" when I stop abruptly. Standing in front of me holding umbrellas are three people: a young woman, a young man, and an older woman.

The young woman asks in English, "Are you the American looking for family?"

"Yes."

"We are your family. May we come in?"

With my mouth hanging open, I stare at her. I suspect my stunned expression concerns her, as she says hesitantly, "We are your family. We have proof. We have pictures and documents. May we come in?"

I get my senses about me as I step aside. "Of course, come in." My heart starts racing, while butterflies flutter in my stomach. Anticipation fills me. Eager to hear what they have to share, I invite them to sit at the dining table.

The young woman starts, "My name is Marinella. This is my boyfriend, Gianluca, and my mother, Loredana. My father is Ugo. Donatella told us you were looking for family, so we had to come meet you. We are Fanti. My grandfather was related to the Fanti you showed Donatella, but my grandmother is related to Bacca. My great-grandmother was Angela Bacca."

"Angela Bacca! I think that was my grandfather's niece. I have a copy of a letter she wrote to my grandfather." From there we talk, share pictures, and look at letters and documents for over two hours. Gianluca and Loredana do not speak English, so we keep Marinella very busy translating for everyone. I discover Angela was the daughter of Giovanni, my grandfather's brother. My great-grandfather was also Giovanni, as was Angela's brother; and then there is Giovanni, the nephew. Giovanni Bacca is obviously a popular name.

I learn about Angela's children, discovering her son, Carlo, is still living in Rumo with his daughter and son-in-law who are about to have twins. I am overwhelmed.

There is a picture of an Angela Bacca in the book that Donatella had loaned me. I confirm that she is Marinella's great-grandmother, who was a midwife and had delivered most of the older people in Rumo. I take detailed notes on everything they tell me in order to review it all later.

At one point, Marinella asks, "What can you tell me about the woman in the photo you showed Donatella?"

"Well, her name was Candida Fanti. She was married to Nicolò Bacca. For many years I had no idea my grandfather had a brother named Nicolò. My family had told me he had a brother named William who came to the United States for a while, but not liking it, he returned to Italy. One of my cousins also told me that there was a woman in the family who went by the name of Babe, but that was not her real name. She was unclear who Babe was—a cousin, a sister maybe. She believed that Babe lived in New York.

"Many years later, I was in New Mexico visiting family when a cousin said a man had come to his house introducing himself as Alex Bacca, our cousin. My cousin gave me Alex's phone number, so I could call him. When I spoke to Alex, he explained that he was the grandson of Nicolò and Candida. Candida's nickname was Babe. They first lived in New Mexico where his father was born; then moved to Illinois; and then to Detroit, Michigan. To his knowledge, they had never lived in New York. He sent me these photos, along with other documents, including his father's baptism record, which was signed by my grandfather as a witness."

Marinella responds, "It is so interesting that we are related from both this Candida Fanti and Angela Bacca. It is fortunate you learned the information about Candida. My cousin is very interested in family history too. I am excited to share this information with her." Marinella pulls out a picture to show me. "This is Catterina Bacca. She was Angela's sister. She lived in America. Did you know her?"

"Oh, my word! This is Catterina? She looks exactly like my cousin Margaret in New Mexico. I can't believe how much they look alike. No, I never met her. My family told me my grandfather had a cousin named Catterina Bertoli who lived in Pennsylvania, and when my grandfather first came to America, they assumed he stayed with her. I tried searching for her but only in Pennsylvania. In the little brown suitcase was a letter from her to my grandfather. The return address was Oakland, California. She mentioned her husband in her letter.

"When I broadened my search on the internet, including her husband's name, I found several types of documentation. I realized from her age, and from her letter, she was not my grandfather's cousin, but rather my father's cousin. Sadly, by the time I learned this information, she had passed away a couple of months before. I was angry at myself for not thinking to broaden my search sooner. Oakland is only one hour thirty minutes from where I live. I could have easily visited her."

By the end of our visit, we are all exhausted yet thrilled with our discoveries. Marinella informs me that her father wants to meet me; she asks if they can come another day. After they leave, I am so filled with joy. I cannot wait to tell Giorgio what happened. I call him on the phone. "Ciao, Giorgio. You won't believe what happened. I am so happy, Giorgio. I met my family!"

"Glenda, you are talking too fast. I cannot understand you. Is everything OK?"

"Yes, everything is fine. I am very happy."

"OK, then I will come see you tomorrow, and you can tell me your news."

When Giorgio arrives the next day, he laughs at my enthusiasm as I tell him my story. "I think you had a pleasant day yesterday. I have more exciting news for you. Tomorrow evening at five, I will bring another cousin to meet you. His name is Vinicio. His mother was another daughter of Angela's. Then next weekend, his brother Luciano will be here. He lives in Trento but still has a home here. I will see if he can meet with you."

"Oh my God, Giorgio! Thank you. Thank you so much! Finally, I am meeting my family. I can't believe it. My dream is coming true. Thank you, Giorgio."

Chapter Three

THE NEXT MORNING AT BAR LANTERNA, I GIVE DONAtella a huge smile and thank her for sending my family to me. It is a beautiful morning. The sun is out again; the air is crisp with that fresh rain scent. The grass shimmers from the dew on the ground. I sit at my usual table outside. Waiting for my order to arrive, a shadow comes over the table. I look up. The handsome stranger is standing there. In English he asks, "May I sit?" I nod yes. As he sits, I get a whiff of his aftershave. *Oh my, he smells good! Look at those eyes! Not only are they big and brown, they shine like honey in a jar.* He extends his hand, "I am Marcello Dalmasso." We shake hands.

"Piacere. My name is Glenda Bacca."

"You have become famous in Rumo. Everyone here knows the lady who walks the streets and why you are here. Have you found your family?"

"Oh dear, the lady who walks the streets? That does not sound so nice. Yes, the people who live in that house right there across from the bar are my family. I have walked past that house every day since I arrived, never realizing they were family. Then tonight, I will meet another cousin. My friend Giorgio is setting up another visit for me this week. It has been very exciting."

"I am glad you are being successful. You look happy. You

are more relaxed than the first time I saw you, and I noticed you are beginning to speak more Italian."

"I am feeling more comfortable here. I don't know about the Italian. I try with Donatella because she is very patient with me. I speak a little with other people one-on-one, but I don't feel comfortable when I am in a group. Also, I am finding there are so many people here who speak English or who want to practice their English that I don't have as much opportunity to speak Italian."

"I see an improvement; keep trying. You will learn it. I too have a difficult time here because of their dialect. Maybe we will learn together. Tell me, why is it so important to you that you find your family here?"

"Well, my father died when I was only five years old. My grandmother had died when my father was a teenager. My grandfather died before I was born. My father had two brothers; therefore, I did have aunts and uncles as well as cousins, but it was a small group of people. My uncles did not seem to know much about my grandfather's childhood or family.

"In comparison, my mother's family was quite large. When we were together, they could tell stories for hours about distant relatives, aunts, uncles, and cousins from all over the place. Somehow, I felt like my family was not complete without knowing more about my grandfather and his family. Family has always been important to me. It's important that I be a part of the lives of my brothers, sisters, nieces, and nephews. I felt like, if my grandfather had family here, I needed to have a connection with them."

As I talk, Marcello nods his head and grins. "That's nice. I hope you can make those connections. I understand that it is your grandfather from Rumo who went to America. When did he go?"

"He actually went twice. He went in 1892 and stayed until 1896. Then he returned to Italy until 1899, at which time he moved permanently to America."

"Interesting. You said your father died when you were five. Do you have any memories of him?"

"Not many. When I was three, my baby brother was born. I remember going in the car to the hospital with my dad to pick up my mom and the baby from the hospital. He said to wait in the car until he came back. Then I recall one day playing in our backyard. We had steps with a handrail. I was hanging from the rail when my dad came over to tell me to be careful that I did not hurt myself.

"I remember the night he got sick. He had come home from work. My mom was fixing dinner. My dad sat down to watch TV and relax. While I sat on his lap, my mom told me to move because daddy did not feel well and was going to lie down. Then the doctor came; they sent my dad to a hospital in Albuquerque, the biggest city in New Mexico. We stayed at my aunt's house. One day my mom took all of us to the hospital when she went to see my dad. We could not go in, so we played on the grass outside his room. Pretty soon he came to the window in order to wave at all of us. That was the last time I saw my dad."

"That is sad, and very personal. Thank you for sharing that with me. Do you know anything else about your father?"

"Well, I know that he was a mechanic who owned his own garage in Dawson, the town he was born in, and later in Raton where we lived. He could speak and write Italian, which unfortunately never got passed down to any of his children. My father was in World War II. He was trained as a radio technician, installing and repairing radios on airplanes, but he also drove a diesel truck for the army; at times he repaired the engines on Jeeps and trucks.

"My father was fifteen years older than my mother—in his forties when they met and married. My mother's family owned the restaurant and bar in Dawson. In 1950, when the town was being dismantled, my father stayed to help disassemble some of the machinery. He came into the restaurant late one night at about ten as my mom was cleaning up. He wondered if there was any way he could get something to eat. My mom fixed him a hamburger; it was love at first sight."

"So interesting, Glenda. It is too bad you did not get to know your father. Besides looking for family, what else have you done since you have been here?"

Chuckling, I say, "Other than walking the streets of town? My friend Giorgio invited me to go on a little walk one day with him and his wife, Wanda. We drove to this town called Sanzeno. We parked and started down a path leading to a map. Giorgio showed me that we were walking from Sanzeno to San Romedio, a fifty-minute walk according to the sign. The path we were on used to be an old irrigation system; however, with newer systems, they converted this into a path for walking.

"On one part of the walk, you look out at the valley and see a gorgeous view of apple orchards. On another part, as you look down over the rail you can see way below into the canyon. Oh, on one section the side of the mountain juts out over the path, causing you to duck down and waddle under the ledge.

"When we finished the path, we walked up a road a short distance, discovering these steps going up the hill to San Romedio where you find this unique sanctuary.

It is like five small churches, one built on top of the other. We climbed the steps to see each church. Along the walls are testimonials of miracles that happened in people's lives: a child with a severe illness who survived, a person in a terrible car accident who was not hurt. They are thanking God for the miracles in their lives. It was a moving experience.

"Of course, then we had to walk fifty minutes back. For me, this was not exactly a little walk. I am terribly out of shape, but this is precisely the kind of thing I want to do to get back in shape. If you have never been to this place, you really should go."

"Many people in Northern Italy are hikers. I suspect your friend walks for several hours in the mountains, so for him it probably was a little walk. I have never been to this place. Maybe one day you can take me."

I nod at his comment. "Oh, Giorgio also invited me to go on a walk with him and two of his friends, Roland and Alessio. Giorgio said I could do it because it was a flat walk to Malga Revò, then from there to Proves. I did do it. It was not a difficult walk at all. However, when we started the walk, we were going up an incline, not exceedingly steep, yet still an incline. I asked Giorgio, 'I thought this was a flat walk.'

"He looked at me funny, saying, 'It is flat. Why you think it is not flat?' When I explained it was going uphill, not straight, he gave me the strangest look and said, 'Glenda you are in Northern Italy in the Alps. Of course, it goes up. Everything here goes up and down. Mountains are not straight. Are you crazy!'

"I replied to him, 'I know that. So, why did you say it is flat? What did you mean?'

Giorgio replied, 'It is flat. It is a clean walk. There are no rocks to climb or logs to go over.' At this point, I realized he was saying it was a cleared path." Marcello laughed heartily.

"Then, a few minutes later, Giorgio says, 'Glenda, quiet feet.' I had no idea why he said that, but I told him OK, attempting to walk quietly without stomping my feet. A few minutes later he said again, 'Quiet feet, Glenda. My father always said quiet feet make the distance.'

"Again, I had to ask him, 'What do you mean quiet feet make the distance?'

"He explained, 'If you have quiet feet, you can walk all the way without getting tired.'

"Then I realized he meant slow down; I was walking too fast. As a result, I slowed down, and the next thing I knew they were far ahead of me. I had to practically run to catch up. I think I am learning more English expressions in Italy than Italian.

"I had so much fun with these crazy boys. Roland and Alessio do not speak any English. Still, I enjoyed watching their interactions with each other and with Giorgio. They would tease, joke, and laugh at each other. At one point, Alessio and Roland took off their shoes so they could walk in a trough full of water, acting like little boys."

Marcello is chuckling with a gleam in his eyes. "My father would say the same thing to me. When I was young, I had a great deal of energy. I would run ahead, then run back. He was right. I would get so tired we had to stop. As I got bigger, I learned to pace myself. My father loved to hike. I never went on the long nine-hour hikes with him or climbed to the top of glaciers, but I do like to walk in the mountains." After a pause Marcello asks, "I need to go, but before I leave, I am wondering if you have been to any of the castles in the area?"

"No, not yet. I would like to go see some. I hear there are several castles around here."

"My friend told me about a castle in the town of Merano called Trauttmansdorff Castle. He said that in addition to the large castle there is a massive garden that has spectacular views of the area. I would like to go see it, but I prefer not to go alone. Would you like to go with me?"

I take a deep breath. *I don't even know this man. Is it safe to go with him?* Marcello can sense my hesitation. "I promise I am an honorable man. I will see you safely home again. You do not know anybody here. You must be a trusting person to come all this way and meet all these strangers. You can trust me too. Why not?"

He is right. I didn't know Giorgio either except via email when I got in a car to ride with him from Verona to Rumo. I cannot expect Giorgio and Wanda to be the only ones to take me around the area. "I would love to go. Why not!"

"Good. Will Thursday be OK? I will meet you here at the bar at eight for breakfast before we go."

"OK, I will see you Thursday."

Marcello leaves, and after a few minutes, I pack up my things and go inside to pay for my breakfast. Donatella smiles from ear to ear. "Marcello paid."

Chapter Four

THURSDAY IS ANOTHER PRETTY MORNING. THE SUN IS shining, the air is crisp, and there is a cool breeze. It is going to be a perfect day to go on an outing. I meet Marcello at Bar Lanterna for breakfast as planned.

"Buongiorno, Marcello. Isn't it a lovely morning? A perfect day for an adventure. By the way, thank you for paying for my breakfast the other day. Today, I will pay for breakfast. Fair is fair."

Marcello nods but does not say anything. When I go into the bar to pay for our breakfast, Donatella says, "Marcello paid."

"What! How could he have paid? He has been sitting outside." Donatella laughs, shrugs her shoulders, and walks away. *Mm, I will have to pay for lunch or dinner.* Marcello smiles when I walk out. We head toward the car.

As we reach the bottom of the mountain from Rumo, we turn left, going north from Val di Non into the next valley, Val d'Ultimo. What a gorgeous drive with curvy roads, majestic trees with the sun popping through the branches, blue sky, and streams along the road.

Marcello shares with me some history of the area. "You know you are in the Trentino-Alto Adige region of Italy. All of this region was at one time part of Austria. Rumo is in the Trentino province. When we entered Val d'Ultimo, we entered the Alto Adige province, or often referred to by the people here as Sud Tyrol. Bolzano is the major city of this province. You will see German along with Italian on the signs. The buildings will have a more Austrian or German style to them. The primary language spoken here is German, but of course the younger people also speak Italian, as this is now part of Italy."

"Yes, that is why my family said my grandfather was born in Tyrol, Italy. They must have spoken Italian in Rumo before it actually became part of Italy because my grandfather spoke Italian, and letters written to him were in Italian, though he did have one friend who wrote to him in German. I wonder if most people in Rumo could speak both Italian and German?"

"Maybe. I don't know when exactly people in the area began to speak Italian. So, tell me more about your grandfather. What else do you know about him?"

"Well, in 1892 when my grandfather first came to the United States, he was barely nineteen. The ship manifest said that he was going to Hazleton, Pennsylvania. Perhaps he worked in the coal mines there. The ship manifest for 1899 stated he had been in America previously from 1892 to 1896. It also indicated that my grandfather's destination was Glenwood, Colorado. I don't believe there was coal mining in Glenwood; I am uncertain why he went there.

"The 1900 census records showed he was in Madrid, New Mexico where there was coal mining. My grandfather met my grandmother and married her in Madrid in about 1903. At some point he went to Pueblo, Colorado where he owned some property. He also owned property in Maxwell, New Mexico and near Artesia, New Mexico; however, my grandfather primarily lived in Dawson, New Mexico, which is where my father together with my uncles were born; it is also where my grandparents are buried."

"You actually know a lot about your grandfather, considering you never met him. You have talked about your family, but I have not heard you say anything about a husband or children. Are you married? Do you have children?"

"No, I am—and have always been—single."

"Why not? Why have you never married?"

"Well, it is difficult to answer that. When I was young, I was convinced I would get married. I wanted a large family like mine—five or six children. It never happened. I suspect I am too independent, demanding, stubborn, and selfish. I like to be in control. These are satisfactory qualities for some things but not the best characteristics for a relationship."

"Hmm, you sound like every Italian woman I know. All Italian women are independent, demanding, and like things their way. They are always in control. All Italian men know this and accept it or there would be no marriages in Italy!"

Laughing, I reply, "Well, then maybe I must find me an Italian man."

"What would this man need to be like?"

"Rich of course because I like to spend money; I would prefer to spend his money than mine. He must be very handsome. No woman wants an ugly man! He cannot smoke. It makes everything stink, including the man! He must like wine; it is my favorite drink. Then again, I have learned to like spritzone a lot. Other than that, he must be exceedingly nice and funny."

"I understand why it may be a challenge for you to find the right man!"

"So, Marcello, what about you? Are you married? Do you have children?"

There is a pause. I sense he is hesitant to answer. Finally, he says, "I was married. My wife died in a car accident about four years ago. I have two grown children: a son, Lorenzo; and a daughter, Arianna. My daughter is married with a son two years old."

"I am sorry you lost your wife. That must have been very difficult." Marcello nods his head but doesn't say any more. "From things you have said, I am under the impression you are not from Rumo. Where do you live?"

"I am from Torino in the Piemonte region. My son also lives in Torino with me, but my daughter lives in Chivasso, a small town outside of Torino."

"How far away is Torino?"

"It is about a five-hour drive west of Rumo. It's not too far, and the roads are well maintained. The traffic once you get to Milano can be heavy. Overall, it is a relaxing drive."

"I think my grandmother's parents were from Piemonte. I believe my great-grandfather was born in San Maurizio Canavese and my great-grandmother was born in Leini. Someday, I would like to go visit to see if I can find any record of them. So, what are you doing in Rumo?"

"After my wife died, I had a difficult time adjusting. Last year, I wanted to get away from Torino, so a friend of mine who was born in Rumo suggested I come. He said it would be relaxing and peaceful. He was right. I liked Rumo very much. I come back to visit every once in a while when I need to get away."

I enjoy the mountain scenery as we drive. Nearing our destination, I look out the window and am surprised. "Wow, I did not realize how high in the mountain we are. Are we driving down to that city? It is huge."

Marcello replies, "Yes, that is where we are headed. I am not overly familiar with this area, but from this high up you are not seeing one town. Within a short distance of Merano are at least eight different towns. Merano has a population of about forty-one thousand people, smaller than Trento."

"I am enjoying this trip down the mountain. I like the change in perspective of the area as we get closer and closer. It is interesting to see the buildings get bigger and more defined as we go down." Marcello nods his head in agreement.

We arrive at Trauttmansdorff Castle, park, and begin walking to the entrance. I pause as I examine the castle. Marcello asks, "Are you OK, Glenda?"

"Yes, I am surprised at the appearance of the castle. It does not remind me of a medieval castle with a moat and drawbridge that I see often on TV. It seems more modern, a big rectangular building that brings to mind a Spanish-style hotel you might see in Texas or New Mexico."

"Interesting. I agree it does not look like a medieval castle. I do not know much about the castle myself. Perhaps we will learn more inside."

We do in fact learn later that the castle was first established in 1300 as a small mansion. The Trauttmansdorff family purchased it in the 1500s, with many renovations and alterations done to it since then. I like the term *mansion*. It seems a better fit for the style of the building.

We start our tour in the exhibition area. On display is the history of the area. It is fascinating to see all of the ski paths that were used as transportation from one part of the region to another, as well as how many of them were transformed into roadways or train routes. It is sad to read about the impact that World War I had on this area.

After touring part of the castle, we go out to the gardens. Marcello is right. It is massive. There are four circuit trails and three panoramic trails. It has more than eighty garden landscapes with plants from all over the world. I see the largest white, pink, and rose-colored azalea bushes of my life. The gardens go up the side of a hill; as you walk up, you not only see the expanse of the garden, but you also see the town of Merano as well as the Tessa mountain range. Such a marvelous experience.

On the way home, we stop not far from Merano in a town called Lana for a late lunch/early dinner. We have a typical antipasto dish of cheeses, salami, and pancetta. Then I have a bowl of *canederli*, dumplings filled with cheese and speck, in broth. *Speck* is smoked ham that is incredibly popular in this region. Marcello has polenta with sausage and coleslaw. Marcello is a wonderful conversationalist as we banter about our favorite parts of the castle and gardens.

On the way home, we easily fall back into conversation as Marcello asks me about my hobbies. "When I was younger, I loved going to San Francisco to the theater, symphony, opera, and museums. I don't go much at all anymore. When I do, it is to the theater. I love musicals. I would also go wine tasting in Napa Valley, but now there are many wineries much closer to me. I enjoy gardening. I have a large yard with many different flowers. Not as big as the garden we saw today. I like to read mysteries, historical fiction, and romances mostly. I'm not big on nonfiction. What about you?"

"Cars have always been my interest. I have worked for Fiat in Torino for many years. I will be retiring in the fall. When I was young, I liked to work on cars, go to car races. As a boy, I hiked with my father and played soccer. Italy is full of history, so of course I enjoy going to museums or other historical sites. Before our kids were born, my wife and I traveled some. After I retire, I would like to travel more."

We complete our trip talking about places we have visited, in addition to other travels we would like to experience. Marcello is surprised to hear that I have been to many places in Europe. As he drops me off at my apartment, Marcello inquires, "Would you like to go with me Saturday to a place called Rio Sass Canyon?"

"That sounds nice. Saturday evening my cousin Marinella and her boyfriend, Gianluca, invited me to dinner. They want to take me to their favorite restaurant, Nerina, in Malgolo. You are welcome to come with us, provided you let me pay this time."

Marcello chuckles. "OK."

For some reason, I don't believe he is going to allow me to pay. We agree to meet at the bar again on Saturday morning at eight.

Chapter Five

ON SATURDAY, MARCELLO AND I DRIVE TO THE TOWN of Fondo, about thirty minutes east of Rumo. We park by a lake, Lago Smeraldo. It is a small lake with emerald green water. We walk all around the lake until we come to steps that go down into the canyon. There we find a river, which we stroll along, relishing the peacefulness brought on by the isolation, rippling sounds of the water, the cool mist in the air, and birds chirping. When we come to the center of the city, we find the municipal office to pay for our tickets.

While we wait for our tour guide, we read a paper giving information about the canyon. Fondo is actually built over the canyon. This tour will take us below the city down three hundred steps into the canyon. That means coming back up three hundred steps. *That's a lot of steps! I hope my knees and legs can hold out.* It is fascinating to read how the canyon was formed over the years by the Rio Sass river that still flows through it.

Our tour guide arrives, leading us to a building where we suit up for the excursion. Everyone has to wear a red hard hat with a yellow raincoat. Marcello and I laugh at how adorable we are in our new outfits. Entering the canyon, we are on a grated walkway. I feel safe, provided I have handrails to clutch, as I avoid looking down between the slats in the walkway. The light varies along the walk from being very bright to rather dark. At one point, it is so dark I get nervous and turn on the flashlight on my cell phone to see the steps in front of me. There are places where the passage is extremely narrow, requiring one to go sideways along the walkway.

As we arrive at the bottom of the canyon, there is an open area with picnic tables. Our guide informs us we will take a break here before finishing the tour. Marcello asks, "Are you enjoying the canyon, Glenda?"

"Certo. I did get a little nervous a couple of times when it was really dark. I am glad I had my flashlight. Given how narrow some of the passage is, I understand now why they discourage you from wearing a large backpack."

"Yes, I agree. The section where the rocks are red from the algae in contrast to the green from all the foliage around it was spectacular. Also, the narrow point in the walk when we looked up and saw the road above us with the city trees overhead helped me to understand just how far under the city we had gone."

"It is an amazing tour. I like this area too with the picnic tables. I would not mind having a picnic in an area like this. Thank you so much, Marcello, for bringing me on this journey."

"You are welcome, Glenda. Thank you for coming with me. Looks like our guide is ready to head back."

After our tour, we stop at a local bar for a light lunch. Upon returning to Rumo, we part ways for the afternoon, meeting up again with Marinella at seven to drive to Malgolo for dinner. Marinella is riding with us. Gianluca will meet us at the restaurant. Upon arriving at the restaurant, I introduce Marcello to Gianluca. As they shake hands, Marcello says, "Thank you for allowing me to join you this evening."

"It is our pleasure to have you with us. Marinella and I love this restaurant. We are pleased to share it with new friends."

As we enter the restaurant, we receive a warm greeting by a cheerful gentleman who will serve as our waiter. Nerina is a family-owned business; our waiter is one of the sons of the owner. He proudly explains that all of the food prepared is either grown in their own garden or purchased through local vendors; no food or wine is brought in from outside of the region. He then helps us select an exceptional wine that will complement anything on the menu, of which he spares no detail, describing every item.

Our waiter suggests we begin with an antipasto of various meats served with warm bread. The first course of homemade pasta with fresh herbs and lemon is superb. For the second course, I have roast beef seasoned with rosemary. I love rosemary, so it is the perfect dish for me. Dessert is a fabulous cheesecake.

Throughout dinner, Marinella and I talk about family, while Gianluca and Marcello banter on about cars. When I ask for a cappuccino, the waiter laughs. "You must be American. Only Americans would ask for a cappuccino after dinner, but for you, I will make one."

Marinella explains, "In Italy you never drink cappuccino after noon. It is a morning drink only. After noon, one should drink espresso or macchiato."

"I will have to work on that because they are way too strong for me." Everyone laughs.

As dinner comes to an end, I realize we had been there for three hours. Like us, other patrons are socializing over coffee and grappa and enjoying the relaxing atmosphere. Unlike American restaurants where they often rush you out by bringing you the check so they can seat another round of customers, here you are encouraged to visit as long as you want. The waiter will not bring you the check until you request it.

When the check arrives, I ask about the tip. Marinella explains, "Here, there is no expectation to tip. Well, actually, in the big tourist cities like Rome, Venice, or Florence it would be expected because they are used to the American tourists who tip; still, in Trentino, it is not expected. If you want to show appreciation for a fine meal, you can give a tip, but usually it is small here. Not like in America."

"I like that. In America there is such an expectation to tip, even if you have had bad service. It has lost all of its meaning as a gratuity to show appreciation for the quality of service, but rather is another part of the bill. I love that the waiter does not bring you the bill until you ask for it. You don't feel rushed. This has been such an enjoyable evening."

As we leave the restaurant, the waiter gives Marinella and me a kiss on each cheek, shaking hands with the men. Outside, it hits me that Marinella came with us but will ride home with Gianluca. We hug goodnight before we go our separate ways. On the drive home, I comment to Marcello, "You and Gianluca had a long talk about cars."

"Yes, he is very knowledgeable about cars. We have much in common. I am glad that I met him. He is a nice young man. He says he does not know English, yet he spoke exceptionally well."

"I think he knows a lot of English. He simply needs to practice more, although I need to take my own advice. I need to stop letting people speak to me in English. My own insecurities in speaking Italian are holding me back from really learning the language. I always let fear hold me back. I need to be braver."

"You will get there, Glenda. Do not give up on yourself. The restaurant was nice. I understand why Marinella likes it. Our waiter was excellent."

"Yes, I liked him very much. The food was scrumptious. I cannot keep eating like this. I will never lose weight or get back in shape if I keep eating this much food."

On the remainder of the ride home, Marcello shares with me some of the differences in the food and wine that are unique to various regions. I learn that he likes to cook. Although he never became a chef, food and cooking are passions of his. Good thing I am not planning on offering to cook for him. I love to eat, but I am not a skilled cook.

"I had a nice day today, Glenda. Thank you for inviting me to dinner with your family. Tomorrow is my last day in Rumo for a while. I must return to Torino to work. In the morning I need to prepare to leave; then I have some business I need to do. I would like to go on one of your walks with you before I leave. Could we meet at about four to go for a walk on Ziro del Lez?"

I agree to meet him for a walk the next day. I usually walk in the morning; this will be different going late in the afternoon. It is a warm spring day, expected to stay light until late, so why not. We start our walk in Mione from Bar Lanterna. We walk up a steep road to Corte Inferiore, going down the road past Bar Podetti. This is another very nice little bar I have been to with Giorgio. Giorgio is friends with Sandra, the owner, who is kind to everyone. All of the young people really like Sandra; as a result, you often find them hanging out at this bar.

We walk down the road to the small church that is visible from my apartment. It is one of five churches in Rumo. We cannot go in, as it is closed off for renovations. We turn and walk back to Bar Podetti and turn onto a street, proceeding to walk up the road some distance to a picnic area. Here we pick up the path, Ziro del Lez. We walk this path across the hill above Rumo. It is extremely quiet with all the tall trees surrounding us. Periodically, there is a break in the trees, allowing us to see parts of the town below.

The path leads us to Lanza, the village in Rumo that is furthest north. In Lanza we are able to go inside the small church. Then we go to the cemetery. "Wow, Marcello. Look at these headstones. There are many names on some of them, and they have pictures next to the names. I am surprised to see that the graves are family plots."

"Yes, this is very common in Italy. So, in America does each person have their own headstone?"

"Yes, at the cemeteries I have been to anyway. Usually there are not pictures of the person either. Of course, many people today are cremated in America, with ashes spread in different locations; there may not be a grave or headstone at all."

"Cremation does happen here, but it is not as common in Italy. If the ashes are spread, I believe there are designated places in which you must spread them; however, most people still place the ashes in the cemetery."

While walking in the cemetery, I notice there are also some headstones with Bacca family names on them. One is the headstone of Giuseppe Bacca and his wife, who I believe to be the son of Giovanni, my grandfather's brother. Marcello explains that there is another cemetery in Marcena. We continue our walk from Lanza, through Mocenigo, past Corte Superiore, to Marcena. We again visit the church first. Even the small churches are elaborate—so breathtaking with their murals, statues, and decorative altars.

The cemetery in Marcena is bigger. We walk past every headstone. I take pictures of any headstone with a Bacca name. Here, I find the headstones for Angela Bacca and her daughters Bice and Olga; as well as Ida, Natalia, and Olivia Bacca, daughters of Giovanni. In addition, I find Giovanni's headstone with his wife, Maria, and his son Livio, together with Livio's wife, Elsa. I am surprised they are all buried here while Giuseppe is in the cemetery in Lanza. I wonder if there is some story or interesting explanation to this. Although it seems a little strange to be fascinated with graves sites, there is also a comfort in knowing I have a connection to my family. It would be difficult to explain to other people.

By the time we finish our walk, it is almost seven. We go to Vecchia Segheria for a spritzone followed by pizza dinner. Angelo, the owner, is pleased to see us. I thank Marcello for the time he has spent with me and wish him well on his trip home. *I am sorry to see him leave. We have developed a nice routine of having breakfast together. He is easy to talk to, and I enjoy the time I have spent with him. Oh well, I am used to being alone. Besides, I need to spend more time meeting family, which is why I came here. If he makes it back to Rumo before I leave that will be nice, but if not, it will be fine.*

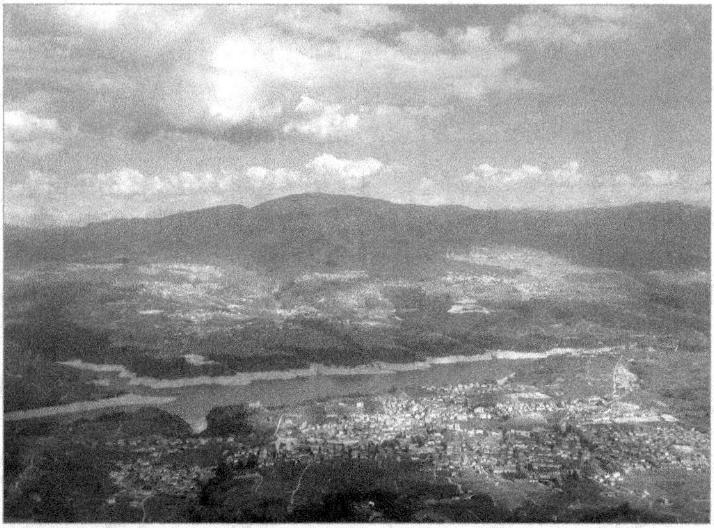

Chapter Six

A COUPLE OF DAYS LATER, I AM COMING HOME FROM my walk. As I approach, I can see a man standing at my door. Giorgio is coming out of the basement of the apartment where he stores work tools plus supplies for his beehives. Seeing me, Giorgio walks up the street to meet me. Giorgio indicates that a cousin is waiting to greet me. He shares that the cousin speaks some English, so I will not have a problem. I am thrilled!

When I get closer to my apartment, my cousin approaches me. "Hello, I am Sergio, your cousin. I was at the grocery store where they told me I had an American cousin staying at Giorgio's apartment. I had to come meet you."

"Hello. I am Glenda Bacca. I am happy to meet you. How are we related?"

"My mother was Ida Bacca, the daughter of Giovanni Bacca."

"Oh, Giovanni was my grandfather's brother. My grandfather was Alessandro Bacca. I know Giovanni had seven daughters and three sons. All of the family I have met so far are related to me through Giovanni. Do you have other family here?"

"My family spent a lot of time in Sweden. I have a brother in Milano, and a brother who still lives in Sweden. My brother Franco and I are here in Rumo. I must be going because it is lunchtime, and I must fix Franco lunch. He is not feeling well. Can I have your phone number? One day I will call you to set up a day to visit more." We exchange phone numbers, and I thank him for taking the time to come find me. I am elated to have met another member of my family, instantly formulating questions to ask him on our next visit.

On Thursday, Giorgio and his friend Alessio are at the apartment when I return from a walk. They are doing some work on their beehives. Giorgio invites me to go with them in the afternoon to Mt. Peller to hunt for *insalata di orso*—bear salad. I have no idea what he is talking about, but why not! I love adventures!

The elevation of Rumo is about three thousand five hundred feet. Going to Mt. Peller, we go up about another three thousand feet. Where we park, there are wildflowers in bloom on one side of the road, while on the other side there is still snow on the ground. Giorgio and Alessio put on their hiking boots. They traipse all around, searching for *insalata di orso*. I walk mostly along the road, admiring the flowers while taking pictures of the mountain range around us.

When Giorgio returns, he hands me two little plants that look like miniature asparagus. He indicates they are *insalata di orso*, but they are too little. Giorgio and Alessio will come back after the snow melts to look again. He explains that you cook the insalata in water, then put them in vinegar. *Hmm, it sounds like pickled asparagus.*

As we go back down the mountain, Giorgio points out a volcano that last erupted hundreds of years ago. Then we stop at this perfect spot with a breathtaking panoramic view of Val di Non. It is a clear, refreshing day, and you can see the entire valley from here as well as the mountains that surround the area. Giorgio points out Rumo from where we stand. Giorgio teaches me the Italian word for breathtaking: *mozzafiato*! Our little trip ends with a stop at a gelateria that makes their own gelato. Delicious!

About three weeks have passed since Marcello left for Torino; it has been a busy time. It is nearing the end of May. I have already been here over a month. Giorgio and Marinella often ask me if I have seen or heard from Marcello. I shrug my shoulders, replying, "He lives in Torino. Why would I hear from him?"

I do not dare tell them I can't stop thinking about him. I often hope I will see him as I walk up to the bar. I wish he was with me when I take my walks. I wonder what he is doing, who he is seeing. Then I tell myself, *STOP! He lives in Italy, and I live in America. I cannot get involved with him.*

Of course, just as I am forgetting about him, I am walking up the main road from Marcena to Mione when a car horn honks. As I turn, I see Marcello, causing my heart to skip a beat. I can't help but beam from ear to ear. Marcello greets me, "Hello. Where are you going?"

"I had lunch at Giorgio and Wanda's. I am walking home."

"I need to go drop off my things at my apartment. I could meet you at Bar Lanterna for a refreshment in about twenty minutes if you do not have other plans."

"Great. See you there." As he pulls away, I take a deep breath. *Oh, dear Lord, why? Why do you introduce me to a man like this when you know I live thousands of miles away! I have to remember he is simply a friend. Nothing more can come of this.*

Marcello is at the outside table when I arrive. Donatella comes out to take our order. She has a huge smile, an eyebrow slightly raised, and a twinkle in her eye. I have to look away before my face turns all red. I order peach tea. Marcello has not yet eaten lunch, so he orders a salad with lemonade. I inquire of Marcello, "How long are you here for this time?"

"I am here through the weekend. I have to return on Monday morning. It is a short visit, but I wanted to get out of the city. OK, tell me about the family you have met since I was here last."

"Well, you know I met Marinella, her mother, and Gianluca. I did then meet her father, Ugo. He is a nice man with a good sense of humor. He speaks to me purely in Italian, which is good. I don't often understand most of what he says, but if he speaks slow enough and gestures enough, I can sometimes get his message.

"Ugo is a talented photographer. He gave me a thumb drive with amazing pictures he has taken all over the area. I also met his son, Gabriele. He is a handsome young man who, as I understand it, is an outstanding soccer player. They took me to pizza one night at that restaurant we saw by Lago Smereldo in Fondo."

"Yes, I remember seeing that restaurant. Undoubtedly, it was delicious. All pizza in Italy is tasty."

I chuckle. "Yes, it was very good. I told you before that I met a cousin, Vinicio. Well, his brother Luciano finally came for a weekend, and Giorgio was able to take me to his house in Lanza to interpret for me while we visited. He and his wife were welcoming. Luciano is currently president of the Rotary club in Trento, and I am a member of Rotary in America, so he is going to find a date when Giorgio can bring me to a meeting. That will be interesting to attend a Rotary meeting in Italy. Luciano gave me a fabulous gift, a set of newspapers that covers one hundred years of Trentino history, starting about 1913. They are all in Italian, so I have another reason I must learn Italian."

"That was exceptionally kind of him. That will be a perfect way to improve your Italian, as well as learn the history of the area. I will be happy to help you with some of the interpretation if you need it."

"Thank you. Then one day when I came home from a walk, there was a cousin waiting to meet me. His name is Sergio and he lives in Marcena. We couldn't talk long, as his brother was waiting for him. We haven't spoken again yet. Then a couple of days ago, Giorgio told me he ran into a cousin of mine in Cles named Luigi. He arranged for me to have dinner with Luigi along with his daughter Anna next Tuesday. Anna speaks English, and she will interpret for her dad. I am excited to meet them."

"This is good news, Glenda. I am happy you have met more of your family. What about the people you were told live in your grandfather's house, the Bacca house as you call it? Have you met them yet?"

"No. I understand from Marinella that a man named Elio lives in the house; sometimes he is here at the bar because he is the boyfriend of Donatella's sister, Luisa. I have not seen him here yet. Giorgio also told me he let Elio know I am here, but he and Giorgio have both been too busy to decide a time for us to meet. Giorgio promised me it will happen one day soon. I guess the other people who live in the Bacca house have other homes elsewhere. They only come in the summer to Rumo. Maybe in June, I will meet them."

"Well, I will look forward to hearing all about it when you meet. If you do not have plans for the weekend, I have some ideas of things we can do."

I take a deep breath to calm the butterflies that flew into my stomach. "I have no plans. What are your ideas?"

"I was thinking that tomorrow, since you like wine so much, we could do some wine tasting; then on Sunday, we could go to a lake. There are a couple of lakes not far from here. We can decide later which lake we want to go to."

"Wine tasting is always a pleasurable activity, as long as one of us stays sober. I do like lakes, but I do not swim. Provided you promise not to throw me in the water, we could visit a lake."

Marcello chuckles. "OK, I promise. I will stay sober, and I will not throw you in the water. I will meet you here tomorrow morning at eight for breakfast, OK?"

"Perfect. See you then."

Chapter Seven

"Buongiorno, Glenda. How are you this morning?"

"Buongiorno, Marcello. Sto bene, grazie. I am looking forward to today. Do you have a specific plan, or is it going to be a day full of surprises?"

"If there are any surprises, I hope they are good ones. I made reservations for us for a tour of Mezzacorona winery about forty-five minutes from here. Then we can visit a little of the town after we have lunch. In the afternoon, I would like to visit a couple of wineries in San Michele, not far from Mezzocorona. Does that seem OK?"

"Yes, sounds nice. Mezzacorona wine is easily purchased in America. I have had their Pinot Grigio many times. It will be fun to see the winery. What a nice opportunity."

Following our little breakfast, we start our drive to Mezzocorona. Marcello, as usual, is full of questions, and I seem to do most of the talking. "Glenda, you told me about the family you met. What else did you do while I was gone?"

"I had so many adventures! First Giorgio and Alessio took me with them hunting for *insalata di orso*. I had never heard of it. It was like a little asparagus that they pickle to eat as antipasto. Then, one day, Giorgio took me to Lago di Tovel. Oh, you said something yesterday about going to a lake tomorrow. If you want to go to Lago di Tovel, I am happy to go again."

"It is nice to know that you have been there, but there are other lakes. Maybe tomorrow we can go to the lake at Molveno. Have you been there?"

"No, I will be happy to go."

"OK. Tell me about Lago di Tovel."

"Oh, it was ideal. There were few people there. Giorgio said in the summer months it will be full of people. We went at the right time. It was very quiet and peaceful. It had clear blue-green refreshing water. You could see the Dolomiti mountains all around. At the top of the mountains, there was still snow. The reflection of the mountains on the water was absolutely stunning. It is not a huge lake, yet much bigger than Lago Smereldo in Fondo. Giorgio took me on a trail that went around the entire lake. Apparently, the water used to turn red in the late spring and summer. Giorgio told me of the legend of a princess who did not want to marry a prince from another village, so she killed herself. The water turning red was a reminder of her sad death."

"Legends are always fun to hear. I suspect the scientists have a different explanation for the red water."

"Yes, something about the algae in the water, I think. Today there is less algae, so the water does not turn red anymore. I like the legend better!"

"Me too. Is that all you have done?"

"No, I was incredibly busy while you were gone. The next big event was attending my first Italian birthday party. Every year, Giorgio and his friend Roland celebrate their birthdays together. It started at noon, continuing until dark. Their best friends were there. I did not realize I had not met all of their best friends yet. At the party I met another couple, Luigino and Maria Luisa. Also, at the party were Sandro, Giorgio's son; his girlfriend, Laura; and Giorgio's sister, Carla, and her husband. I met Wanda's sister, also named Carla; and her niece Lorenza with her husband and daughters. Lorenza speaks English, so she sat by me to visit as well as to interpret for me.

"Roland grilled turkey, bacon, sausage, steak, and polenta. The women had made antipasto platters of salami, pancetta, prosciutto, cheeses. Then, they served salads in addition to vegetables of potatoes, zucchini, peppers, and beans. Every time I looked down, someone had added more food to my plate. Of course, we had plenty of wine. Then there were cookies for dessert followed by champagne, gifts, and singing.

"In the late afternoon, Sandro and Laura took me to Trento to pick up my niece Sarah with her boyfriend who had come to visit me. When we got back, people started eating again for dinner. Then came the big birthday cake, which was made by Liliana, Alessio's wife. Oh my gosh, it was such a scrumptious cake. Don't forget the grappa. They were really welcoming to Sarah and her boyfriend. We had so much fun."

"It sounds like a typical Italian celebration. Always lots of food and drink, mixed with laughter. I like hearing you tell your stories. You are full of joy with a big smile and shiny eyes. Your voice gets louder with more inflection when you are excited. It is like a child. You have a young heart, a young spirit."

"My sister Becky used to tell me I had a young soul, a youthful way of looking at things. I try to maintain that as I get older. That must be why I love adventures and parties!"

"How nice that your niece came to visit. What did you do with her?"

"Well, they were here about four days. We went to dinner at Hotel Viridis in Cagnò, Hotel Margherita in Marcena, and, of course, pizza at Vecchia Segheria. They rented bikes in order to ride around and explore the area. My niece did a summer program one year in the town of Asolo. She wanted us to see it, so we drove there for a visit. It was the first time I had driven very far out of Rumo. Giorgio loaned me his GPS so I would not get lost. Then we went to Venice and spent one night. The weather was not the best. It rained most of their visit. Even in Venice, we had to walk around with our umbrellas open much of the time, but we still had a wonderful time together."

"Four days is a short visit. It is generous of you to host them. I trust they enjoyed their time. I wish I had been able to meet them. Well, here we are. Are you ready for wine?"

"Certo!"

The tour at Mezzacorona is in English. We learn that this plant is one of three the winery owns. They also have one in Southern Italy and one in Central Italy. This plant is enormous, with a facility for making table wine in addition to a plant for sparkling wine. They produce three million bottles of sparkling wine a year, combined with forty-three million bottles of table wine. I tell Marcello that I recall Giorgio's brother-in-law works for Mezzacorona. He told me the winery sells a large amount of wine to Gallo Winery in Modesto, California near where I live. It's a small world! I buy several bottles of wine; there is plenty of time to drink this before I leave Italy.

After our tour, we go into town. The town is surrounded by the Mezzocorona mountains. We take a tram up to the top of the mountain. What a view! You can see the winery, massive vineyards, apple orchards, and the town below as well as surrounding towns, including Trento. We find a little bar where we eat lunch, then take the tram back down to walk around the center of the town where we go into a church and a couple of stores.

Leaving Mezzocorona, we drive to San Michele not far away. There is a specific winery Marcello wants to visit, but we can't locate it. We end up driving up a hill on a winding road. As we come around one curve, we see a sign that says "Bellaveder—Open," so we turn in. All around the winery, you can see rolling hills covered with green grapevines. The building is large, and we debate which way to go. With only one other car in the parking lot, it is questionable if they are actually open. Suddenly, a man appears from one of the buildings greeting us, "Buongiorno. Prego."

Marcello inquires in Italian, "Per favore, possiamo assaggiare il vostro vino?"

"Certo, seguitemi." He leads us to the tasting room, which is quite expansive with tables and chairs.

"Wow, look at the size of this room and the beautiful wood furniture, Marcello."

Upon hearing my English, the gentleman responds, "It is large so we can host special events during the year. You are American? Where are you from?"

"I am from California."

"I hear they have excellent wine in California, but I am sure you will enjoy our wine."

"I have no doubt. I am excited to hear all about your wine as we sample it."

The gentleman is thrilled to share with us information about their wine, as well as wines in the region. He welcomes any questions we have. He shows us a book of award-winning wineries in Italy. He opens it to the page with Bellaveder listed. Naturally, we have to taste the award-winning wines. I especially enjoy Lagrein and Teroldego; I cannot leave without buying a couple of bottles. As we are purchasing our wine, Marcello asks, "I was looking for a specific winery in San Michele, but we could not find it and spotted this place as we came up the hill. Are we still in San Michele?"

"No, you are in Faedo. If you are looking for another winery to visit, I recommend you continue up the hill to Pojer e Sandri. They have excellent award-winning wines. You will be very pleased with their offerings."

We thank him for his hospitality as we head on our way.

"I love when something fun and unexpected happens! What a delight that was. I must find a copy of that book."

"Oh, Glenda. I think you love everything, especially wine!"

We have no trouble finding Pojer e Sandri winery. Since we had red wines at Bellaveder, we decide to do white wines. My favorite is Nosiola, a refreshing white wine that is not too dry yet not too sweet. It is a varietal grown specifically in the Trentino region. By the time we finish here, we have had enough wine to drink. Marcello shakes his head at the amount of wine I am taking home. "I think you must truly like Italian wine, Glenda."

"Yes, I do. They are different than many of the wines I drink in America, especially the red wine. I have not seen an Italian wine with more than twelve percent alcohol content. In America, most red wine seems to range from thirteen to sixteen percent. Also, many red wines are high in tannins, making them more bitter than I like. I have not had a bitter red Italian wine yet."

"Interesting. I will have to come to America to try your

red wine sometime. Are you ready for a late afternoon snack?"

"Absolutely. Why not!"

Marcello drives us to the town of Lavis not far away. We go to an ice cream parlor that makes their own gelato. You can get a cone, but they also have a large menu with a variety of specialty dishes like banana splits and sundaes. Some of them are huge—big enough for two or three people to share. I can't resist. I must have a large sundae with coffee ice cream and lots of chocolate syrup with whipped cream. Yum, yum! Marcello has a sundae with *nocciola*, hazelnut, ice cream. It is a very popular item in Italy but not my favorite flavor at all. We enjoy our treats as we recap our favorite parts of the day.

Chapter Eight

Sunday morning, I wake up late. I had slept poorly. I had not been able to go right to sleep, then tossed and turned throughout the night. I had ongoing conversations about Marcello in my head. *He is so kind, funny, and handsome. He is easy to talk to. I think he likes being with me too. Seriously though, I cannot fall for this guy. I do not want to have just a fling. Yet I cannot fall in love with him. I live in America. I have family and friends who need me. I have a house and responsibilities. I know how to maintain a friendship with a man; that is all I will have with Marcello. I must keep my feelings under control!*

Marcello picks me up at nine. It is another sunny day, with the temperatures expected to be in the mid-70s. The scent of freshly mowed grass fills the air. There is a possibility of rain in the late afternoon, so I bring a sweater as well as my raincoat if needed.

As we head to Molveno, Marcello shares, "I have never been to Molveno, but I have heard much about it. It is very much a tourist town. Lago di Molveno is the major attraction to the town in the summer. It is one of the largest lakes in the Trentino region. It is partially surrounded by the Dolomiti mountains. I understand that at one time Molveno and the nearby town of Andalo were dying communities. Then the German tourists discovered it for skiing and loved it. Today there are many Germans, as well as other visitors, who come every year for skiing, which is the major attraction in the winter."

"Interesting. I do not swim nor do I ski. I will be happy to walk around the lake and in the mountains. Now that I know there is a town, maybe I can do some shopping. I cannot go home without some gifts."

"A typical woman—loves to shop. I am sure we can find time for that."

"OK, Marcello. I usually do most of the talking as we drive. I think today it is your turn. Tell me about yourself, your family, your childhood, what you did the past few weeks?"

"Well, as for the past few weeks, I worked, saw my children, and went to dinner with some friends. No new adventures like you. For you, everything was new and exciting. For me, it was just day-to-day life. As a child, I grew up in the town of Domodossola, Italy. It is a small town in the northernmost part of Piemonte region, in the Verbano-Cusio-Ossola province. It is at the foot of the Alps, with an elevation of about three thousand eight hundred feet.

"When I was growing up, it was smaller, about ten thousand population. Today, I think it is closer to eighteen thousand people. It has a major railway station that allows people from Switzerland and Italy to travel easily between the countries. It also provides for commercial transportation between Switzerland and Milano. Of course, what I remember about it as a child is playing in the mountains, hiking with my dad, and skiing in the winter. I had a lot of fun there as a child."

"If it is that close to Switzerland, did you learn to speak German growing up?"

"My primary language is Italian, the main language of the area. I did choose to also learn German and over the years spent much of my time in Switzerland."

"Wow, you are fluent in three languages. Impressive."

"In Europe, it is not uncommon for people to be fluent in at least two languages, often three, because of all the travel and connections to other European countries. These days, in many countries, children in school are also taught English. I actually learned English when my children started to be taught English in school. I didn't want them saying bad things about me that I did not understand!"

"You're funny. What about your family? Brothers, sisters?"

"My parents lived in Domodossola until they died. I have some cousins still living there. I have two brothers and two sisters. One sister still lives in Domodossola, while one lives in Milano. My oldest brother lives in Switzerland. My younger brother lives in Germany. I don't see any of them often. Maybe when I retire, I can spend more time visiting with them. I left Domodossola when I went to college in Milano. I met my wife there. When we finished school, we went to Torino so she could be near her family. My children grew up knowing their mother's family more than mine. They are very tied to the Torino area."

"Thank you for sharing that with me." Marcello nods. I can see from a road sign that we are entering Andalo. Molveno is not far. One of the things I love about Northern Italy is that every place I go, the area is clean and fresh looking. Even the old buildings are clean and well maintained. Driving through Andalo, you can see the style of buildings is more German, with pitched roofs with exposed wooden beams. There are several little shopping centers along the main road. *It will be fun to come back here to shop.*

Approaching Molveno, we look down the side of the road and can see the lake below us. It takes my breath away. Once we reach the lake, we park, get out, and begin exploring the area. I soon realize this is a perfect lake for tourists. It has paddleboats, hang gliding, bikes for rent, a playground for children, swimming, miniature golf, tourist shops, and restaurants.

We have a delightful time walking around part of the lake. Half a dozen times, Marcello's hand brushes mine. I get tingles up my spine. I wonder if he is going to try to hold my hand. *That will not be good. We have to remain just friends.*

Marcello points to the mountain. "Look, do you see the ski lift going to the top of the mountain? Would you like to go for a ride?"

"Yes, that would be nice."

When we pay for the lift tickets, the gentleman explains it is in two parts. You get off halfway up and then get on another lift. However, as we ascend, we see many people hiking up the mountain. Getting off the first lift, Marcello inquires, "Would you prefer to continue on the next lift, or would you like to walk the remainder of the way?"

"Let's walk. I need the exercise." It is a bit of a climb for me, but I succeed. It feels like we are on top of the world. From the top of the mountain, the town and lake appear so small. There is a restaurant where we have a late lunch, enjoying the fresh mountain air.

Walking back down the mountain, Marcello asks, "Glenda, have you ever considered living in Italy?"

This question catches me by surprise. I wonder what prompted it. Taking a deep breath, I reply, "No. I have a home with responsibilities in America. My family and friends are there. I mean, family as in my brothers, sisters, nieces, and nephews. My close family. I have never considered living away from my family. Have you ever thought of living away from your family?"

"I understand what you are saying. No, I have never wanted to live far away from my family. I do think of moving away from Torino. I enjoy the smaller towns with mountains. I would not want to move so far away from my children that I could not see them often. I hope they will never want to move far away from me either."

"I don't know what it would take for me to move to another country. I think of my grandfather—how brave he was to move to America without family. I know the times were different, and people felt they had no choice if they were going to find work to survive. I will never be in that situation, so I don't know if I could leave my family behind."

This conversation leaves us both deep in thought. It is a quiet drive home. Marcello leaves me at my apartment. He will be returning to Torino early the next morning. He believes he will be able to return in a couple of weeks. I know we need to be merely friends, yet I cannot help but be disappointed he is going.

Chapter Nine

It is closer to three weeks, but there he is, sitting at the table drinking a cappuccino and reading the paper. My heart starts racing. In my eagerness to see him, I start walking so fast I am almost running. I know when he sees me, my face is beaming with joy.

"Ciao, Marcello. Welcome back! How was your time in Torino?"

"It was enjoyable. I saw my son and daughter, played with my grandson. It is always a joy to be with my grandson. I went to Milano last weekend to have dinner with my sister and her family. It was my sister's birthday. We had a nice visit. I told all my family about this crazy woman I met in Rumo. They would like to meet her sometime."

"Well, maybe if I ever visit Torino, I can meet all of them. I have no doubt that would be fun."

Marcello shakes his head slightly. "I heard that Donatella went on vacation for a week. What did you do for breakfast?"

"I went to Bar Podetti. Sandra is very nice. She also makes an excellent cappuccino and has yummy pastries. I did, however, miss my view of the valley from here."

Marcello laughs. "I have been anxious to hear about any adventures you have had lately."

"Oh, Marcello, I have had a marvelous three weeks. So much fun!"

"Even without me?"

"When every day is an adventure, it is difficult not to enjoy it regardless who is with you." Marcello shakes his head. I have a feeling in some way I am disappointing him. I do not know what else to say, except to tell him about the past few weeks.

"I went on a hike with Giorgio, Alessio, and Roland again. I believe it was to Monte Ozolo. The first half was an easy walk. When we arrived at this one point, Giorgio said it would be a steep hike for about ten minutes. He believed I could do it; still he did not want to have to call the helicopter to rescue me. I promised him I was healthy and could do it.

"I did OK for a short distance, until I ran out of breath. I had to stop several times. Roland and Alessio went ahead, but Giorgio was very kind to wait for me frequently. It probably took me twenty-five minutes instead of ten, but I did it! I was proud of myself, and it was terrific exercise."

"Brava, Glenda. If you continue to do short little hikes like that, soon you will be able to do longer hikes. Don't give up."

"My next escapade was with Giorgio, Wanda, and all of their close friends. We went on a *passeggiata gastronomica*! I had never heard of such a thing before. When I was young, I was in a girl's youth organization. Sometimes we would have what they called *progressive dinners*. You would have appetizers at one girl's house, then go to a different house for salad, a different house for the main course, and a different house for dessert. It was fun, but the passeggiata gastronomica is better because it is outside and you get to exercise as you eat.

"I don't remember the exact location of this walk. We started near an apple processing plant where we registered, then walked along a mountain path. Along the entire path there were about seven different stations set up with food and drink. The first one had bread with butter or jelly and coffee or tea. The next one was yogurt, apples, and apple juice. At one point it was a full lunch, and then at the end was a dessert station.

"We walked about six-and-a-half miles that day. My friends were a little worried because I looked tremendously tired by the end. I was exhausted, but I was so happy to be with them. They are funny, kind, loving, and giving people. I truly enjoy any time I am with them!"

"I have done a passeggiata like that before. It is an incredible way to spend the day, get exercise, and enjoy the company of others. If I hear of another one, maybe we can go sometime."

"That would be fun. Oh, maybe one day I can take you to hear my friend Giorgio sing in his choir. It is called Coro Maddalene. Giorgio took me to a choir performance one night. It is an all-male choir. I did not understand the words, but the music was mesmerizing. I understand that sometimes they sing at Malga Revò. Maybe if they sing there when you are visiting, we can go for a little hike before or after they sing."

Marcello agrees this is a sound idea. I catch a movement out of the corner of my eye. It is my cousin Marinella coming to join us. We spend an hour or more visiting. At different times, Marinella and Marcello speak only in Italian. I do not mind, as I love to listen to the language. Italian has a musical quality, along with varying rhythm and emphasis on words that make it pleasing to the ear. I don't think they are trying to exclude me—just wanting to talk in their native language. It is a perfect opportunity for me to try, unsuccessfully for the most part, to practice my Italian. At one point, Loredana also stops by, as do some friends of Marinella's. Then, as a man comes up to the table to speak to Marinella, my eyes almost pop out of my head.

Marinella introduces us. "This is my uncle Roberto, my dad's brother."

"Oh, my word, you look exactly like my brother Robert. Let me find a picture."

"Yes, I can see the resemblance. Genetics are an amazing thing. I must go in and visit with some friends, but we will talk more another day."

"OK, ciao ciao."

Marinella states, "I too must leave. I hope to see you again tomorrow. Have a good day. Ciao."

After she departs, Marcello asks, "Who was it that Marinella asked you about?"

"Oh, it was my niece Kortne and her boyfriend, Brian. They came to visit me, and Marinella was able to meet them. We went to visit Castel Thun together. Kortne and Brian were here about four days. One day we went to Florence by train. We visited the Boboli Gardens and the Uffizi museum, and walked around the area.

"Another day, Giorgio and Wanda took us to Innsbruck, Austria. We went to Old Town, the old historical area of Innsbruck. We visited a few shops, then toured the Imperial Court Church. It was fantastic! It is a Gothic church that houses the tomb of the Emperor Maximilian I, one of the most important kings of Tyrol, who died in 1519. If I remember correctly, it was the Emperor's dying wish to be buried surrounded by his ancestors. So, all along the church are about forty lifelike, gorgeous bronze statues of kings and queens.

"Then we went to the top of the mountain where the 1976 Winter Olympics were held. Such a stunning view from the top. What a special day that was, to be together with my new friends and my family."

"Very nice, Glenda. I have been to Innsbruck once in my life. I never saw the Imperial Church. This is another interesting site you have introduced to me. I must go one day."

"It was lovely. Marinella also asked me about Ken and Cindy. They are friends from America who came to visit right after Kortne and Brian. Marinella and Gianluca went to dinner with us at Nerina restaurant. I took Ken and Cindy to San Romedio, Rio Sass Canyon, and Castel Thun. For something different, we went to Lago di Garda. That is a massive lake. I had no idea it was that big.

"We also went to Malcesine, where we visited a castle. The castle was more like a fort, not a castle where people lived as much as a castle that served to protect the area from invaders coming in by water. Then we took the lift up Mount Baldo, elevation seven thousand two hundred seventy-seven feet. What an exquisite view! I had fun showing my friends around the area."

"You are visiting many special places on this vacation. It is nice that your family and friends from America visited you to learn about your grandfather's home."

Suddenly Donatella is standing at our table. She places in front of us plates, silverware, a platter of meats and cheeses, a large salad, bread, and glasses of tea saying "Buon appetito" as she walks away. We both look at our watches. We cannot believe we have sat here all morning visiting. How thoughtful that Donatella brought us lunch!

While we eat, I continue to share my activities over the past three weeks.

"I believe, before you left last time, I had told you that Giorgio scheduled a dinner date for me with my cousin Luigi from Cles with his daughter Anna. They are so sweet! Luigi and Anna invited me to their home for lunch one day. They cooked a feast! Too much food.

"I met Luigi's wife, Luciana; another daughter, Elisa, with her husband, Franco; along with Anna's husband, Simone. I also met Luigi's sister, Lucia; and her husband, Renzo. Then I visited them again at which time I met Luigi's brother, Giovanni, and his wife, and then later his other daughter, Ilaria. They showed me a picture of Luigi's mother, Rosa. She reminded me of my cousins Katherine, Lucille, and Ginger who live in New Mexico."

"Wow, that is a big family, Glenda. You met so many people."

"Yes. Then, Lucia also invited me to her house one day for lunch. I really like Lucia. Her appearance, smile, and friendly manner remind me a great deal of my cousin Carolyn, who lives in New Mexico. I met Lucia's daughter, Paola; her son-in-law, Carlo; as well as her granddaughter Chiara, who speaks English and interpreted for us.

"Lucia is the family historian. I enjoyed all the stories she told me. One story was about how her mother and father met. When her father was ready to get married, a friend told him to go to the Bacca house in Rumo where they had several daughters. He went, pretending that he wanted to buy a cow. Ultimately, he confessed that he did not want a cow, he wanted to find a woman to marry. Rosa, one of the daughters, had seen him through her window and heard why he was there. The mother sent him off saying she would think about it. When the mother came in the house, Rosa told her she wanted to marry the man. I laughed so hard. I had such a delightful time."

Shaking his head and laughing, Marcello says, "Now, that is love at first sight! I think many marriages back then were arranged, but I have never heard a story like this."

"I also learned from Lucia that Catterina, the relative I told you about earlier who lived in Oakland, California, actually came to the United States when she was a teenager. When my grandmother got sick, Catterina was sent to New Mexico to help take care of my grandfather, my father, and his brothers. I am surprised my uncles did not remember more about her. Catterina met her husband and got married in New Mexico; her first child was born in New Mexico. This makes so much more sense to me now. I also learned that one of Giovanni's daughters, Adele, became a nun. I enjoyed learning about my family.

"Of course, I shared with them about my family in America, and the story of my search for my Italian family. Oh, Lucia helped to clarify my grandfather's trips to America. Remember I told you he went twice? She said that she was confident my grandfather returned to Rumo for his brother Giovanni's wedding. It was required that young men at age nineteen serve three years in the army. He had left before serving. Therefore, once he returned, he was required to serve his three years.

"That explains also why I have a picture of him in a military uniform, and the letter in German he received from a friend who had served in the military with him. Lucia was interested in the letters that I found in the suitcase given to me by my cousin. I promised her I would give her copies of them."

"Wow, Glenda, that was a splendid visit. You learned so much. You mentioned the little brown suitcase and these letters before. You said they were in Italian, but you don't know Italian. You must have had them translated."

"Yes, I tried to do it on Google Translate, yet they were not making sense. I could not read the handwriting well enough. A woman who served as a counselor at the high school in the town where I worked agreed to try to translate them for me, including the letter that was in German.

"It took her about three weeks. We met for coffee one day after work. It was one of the most moving days of my life. She did not simply hand me an envelope with the translations. She wanted to talk about them. She told me the letters reminded her of things her mother used to tell her as well: how poor the people were, how they could not afford food or clothes, and how so many had to leave the country to find work if they were to survive.

"She said my grandfather was a very generous man. The letters always thanked him for the money he sent, as well as the food—especially coffee. They thanked him for the clothes, asking him to send any clothes he could, even old and torn, because they could take them apart to remake them into new clothes. We both got tears in our eyes as we talked. Then she read to me every translation of each letter. I was truly blessed that she had agreed to translate them for me."

When I look over at Marcello, he actually has tears in his eyes. *Ah, it warms my heart to see a sentimental man.* "That is a nice story," he says. "We have no idea what it really means to struggle like our ancestors. Hundreds of Italians went to many different countries for work back then. Today, although the economy is better than it was, it is still not the best here. Many young people are leaving Italy to find jobs in other countries today. I wish this would change."

We sit quietly for a few minutes, drinking our after-lunch coffee. Then Marcello asks, "So, you did not take your walk this morning. Shall we take a walk and see what is happening in Rumo today?"

"Why not! That would be great."

"I have things I must do tonight. Tomorrow are you free to go with me to Rabbi?"

"I don't know what Rabbi is, but of course, why not!"

"Then I will surprise you. Wear your trekking shoes, and bring your walking stick."

Chapter Ten

ON THE DRIVE TO RABBI, I SUDDENLY REMEMBER I have not shared some important news with Marcello. I exclaim, "Marcello, I forgot to tell you some fabulous news yesterday."

"Calma, Glenda, calma. Keep calm. Tell me your news." He moves his hand from the steering wheel to the seat next to where my hand is resting. Our fingers touch. Instead of calming down, my heart starts to beat faster.

"One day I was on my walk. I was in Marcena walking toward the park in Corte Superiore. I recognized Giorgio walking toward me. When we met, he told me that my cousin Anita, who lives in the Bacca house, had arrived from Bolzano, and she wanted to meet me. He walked with me to the Bacca house so he could introduce us. When we arrived, Anita was outside with her husband, Mario. Anita and I both started laughing. We explained to Giorgio that a couple of days before while Anita was walking her dog, she and I passed each other on the street. I said "Buongiorno" as I stopped to pet the dog. Anita said she thought I was American and that I looked familiar, but she could tell I did not speak Italian."

"Did you get a tour of the Bacca house?"

"Well, no, not that day. Anita invited me to come to lunch the next day. She said Elio, my other cousin who lives in the Bacca house, would be there too. However, Giorgio could not come; therefore, I would not have anyone to help interpret for me. Giorgio gave me a hard time because he thinks I should be speaking much more Italian by now. He said I need to stop waiting for him or other people to interpret for me. I told him fine, I would come to lunch without him and bring my English/Italian dictionary with me."

Marcello laughs. "Brava, Glenda. I believe many of us speak to you in English because it is a great opportunity for us to practice English. We should stop, but I think it would be extremely difficult for you to tell me all your adventures if you had to do it in Italian. We will continue in English while you tell me about your lunch date with the Baccas."

"I tried to prepare for the lunch date. I looked at what pictures I wanted to share with them, what things I might want to tell them, what questions I had for them, and I tried to anticipate what they might ask me. I looked up words. I wrote out sentences, practicing them out loud. Still, I was very nervous! It went well.

"I was thrilled to meet Elio. Many people had mentioned his name to me. At last, I know who they are talking about. Elio and Mario understand some English, which helped in our communication.

"From the outside, it looks like it is one huge house that they share. I am wrong. It is actually four homes, or in America we would probably call them apartments. I also was under the impression that Elio and Anita were the only Baccas who live there. I was wrong again. I have other cousins who own part of the house, Lino and Ada. They come in the summer, so I probably will not meet them this year.

"I also learned that Anita and Elio have another brother and sister I have yet to meet, Giovanni and Franca. In addition, Mario and Anita have two children, Andrea and Monica, that I would like to meet one day. They live in Bolzano."

"Oh, Glenda. Your family is so big. I will never be able to remember all of them. It is too bad you will not get to meet them all this year. Does that mean you are already planning on returning next year?"

"Oh, probably. Not only to meet them but to meet other family members I have heard about. Maybe I can go to Piemonte to see if I can find information on my grandmother's family. Of course, I would like to see again the friends and family I already know here." Marcello smiles and nods.

"I got a tour of Anita's and Elio's houses. We also went down into a basement where they have a cantina. I loved it! I want a house with a cantina. There were many neat old things down there. They showed me a picture of the Bacca house many years ago. Apparently, it used to be even bigger than it is now. It caught fire one year; when they repaired it, they made it smaller.

"In Elio's house, he has many family pictures. He let me go through them, choosing any I wanted. He is going to scan them and put them on a thumb drive for me. He is really sweet. We also took a picture of Anita, myself, and Elio. When I first met them, I did not think there was much family resemblance, although in the photo I can see a resemblance in our eyes, smiles, and cheeks. I like that I resemble my Italian family.

"Elio also showed me a big trunk that used to belong to my grandfather. It has his name, A. Bacca, on it. It is from when my grandfather was in the military. There is a shelf in it where he would keep his ammunition. My grandfather left it there when he went to America. His brother Giovanni passed it on to his son Livio, who then passed it on to Elio. I love that my grandfather is still represented in the house even though he left."

"You tell delightful stories, Glenda. Did you get to eat any lunch, or did you spend the whole time talking and looking around?"

Laughing, "Of course, you crazy thing. Anita fixed a delicious lunch. She is a fantastic cook like all the women I have met here. She made us a mushroom risotto dish, cantaloupe, pancetta, cheese, bread, and a salad with vegetables from her own garden. I had an absolutely awesome day!"

As we drive, I notice we have gone in a different direction than I have ever been before. I have heard people talk about Val di Sole. I know that Sandro, Giorgio's son, works in Malè in Val di Sole. I watch all of the street signs along the way, noticing signs giving directions to Rabbi. "I assume we are headed to the town of Rabbi. What will we do there?"

"Pazienza, Glenda. Patience. You will see soon enough."

When we reach Rabbi, Marcello continues to drive, turning on a road that goes up into the mountain. We come to a large parking area. We get on a shuttle that takes us to Malga Stablasolo. Marcello suggests we have a cup of coffee and use the restroom before we go on a hike. As we head off, he informs me we will be walking about thirty minutes. It will not be too terribly steep, but it is not flat—there will be some rocks. Not long into our walk, I can hear water flowing. I become so excited.

"Marcello, I hear rushing water. Are we near a river? I love rivers with rushing water. I have learned here in Italy often when there is rushing water there is also a waterfall. I absolutely love waterfalls! Are you taking me to a waterfall?"

"I know you love waterfalls. I remember you telling me Giorgio and Wanda took you to see a waterfall in the Brenta mountains and how much you loved it."

I only have one walking stick. I am glad he told me to bring it, as some of the ground is dangerously uneven with large rocks that are a challenge to step up on. At one point, as I am navigating a large rock, Marcello surprisingly takes my hand. I catch my breath; my stomach does a somersault. Undoubtedly, he is merely helping me up on this rock, but he does not let go. I like the feel of my hand in his. I do not want to let go either. *Surely, he is just being nice. We hardly know each other. I return to America in about a month. Clearly, we cannot have a relationship beyond friendship.*

As we climb, the sound of rushing water grows louder and louder. My anticipation grows as well. We take one last step up, and there it is: a beautiful waterfall with crystal clear water rushing so fast there is a deafening roar coming from the fall. As the water hits the rocks, it makes a loud splashing sound. We stop. I let go of Marcello's hand in order to take pictures. We climb further, as high as possible to get close to the fall. I can feel the mist of the water on my face. It is so cool and refreshing. The tall green trees, the roaring river, the massive waterfall—it is all truly *mozzafiato*! As we head back down, Marcello takes my hand again. Clearly it is because the rocks are wet and slippery. *He is being a gentleman; that's all.*

We eat a little lunch at Malga Stablasolo. Instead of taking the shuttle back to the parking area, we walk back. Marcello informs me he has another place he wants to take me in Rabbi. We drive down the mountain to Rabbi, then take the main road to the northern end of town. Marcello parks again in a large parking lot. "Are you ready for another walk?"

"Yes, why not!"

"We have a choice. We can go back down this road a bit to pick up a cleared path, or we can go to the right and take a path that is steeper, going up the side of the mountain. Which do you prefer?"

"Well, I am not an experienced hiker. I love to be in the mountains, but I usually walk on cleared paths. If you think I can do it, I am happy to go on the steeper path up the side of the mountain."

"I think you can do it. I will help you. If we decide it is too difficult, we can pick up a different path on the way that is easier. Let's go."

It is a very challenging climb for me. Marcello takes my hand again to help me, although I soon let go, using the desire to take a picture as an excuse to stop and catch my breath. We come to a point where you can choose one of two paths. Without a doubt, Marcello chooses the easier of the two for me. It has steps with a railing to help make the climb easier.

Ultimately, we are no longer climbing, but rather walking straight on a path. Soon we come to the end, and in front of us is a suspension bridge going across the canyon. I have never been a particularly brave person, so the idea of walking across this suspension bridge is enormously scary. *How can I not do it? We have come all this way. There are other people walking across it. It must be safe.*

When the other people finish, we start across. I hold tight to the cables as we walk. I know better than to look straight down. When we get to the middle of the bridge, Marcello stops and points. There is the waterfall across from us. "Wow, Marcello, it looks different from what we saw below. It is so far away, you can't hear the rushing of the water. It starts high up on the mountain, appearing long and narrow surrounded by all the trees. It is stunning."

We make it to the other side. I am elated that I have actually done it. "Marcello, this has been a spectacular day. First the waterfall, then the suspension bridge. I have loved every minute of it! Thank you, thank you very much."

"Glenda, you are easy to please. I am glad you have enjoyed the day. Do you want to walk a little more here in the mountain, or are you too tired?" We decide to walk for a bit. Marcello takes my hand again. There is no reason. I do not need help on the cleared path, but I like it, so I do not complain. At times we walk in silence, enjoying the fresh air and peacefulness of the mountain. At other times, we chat. Marcello tells me tidbits about his childhood as well as his children.

We come to another *malga*, an alpine building that provides rest and refreshment for hikers, where we drink a glass of lemonade. By the time we walk back to the car, it is evening. We drive to the center of Rabbi and walk along the river flowing through it, exploring a few stores along the way. Marcello translates a plaque for me that explains the water in the river is thought to have healing powers because of the level of iron that is found in the water. I pass on tasting it. On the way home, we stop in Malè for dinner.

When we arrive home, I am exhausted. Marcello parks his car at his apartment. "I will walk you home, Glenda."

"That is not necessary, Marcello. I feel safe in Rumo, and I am not afraid to walk alone at night."

"I insist. I would not be a gentleman if I let you walk home alone. Let's go."

As we walk down the hill, Marcello takes my hand again. When we reach my apartment, I say goodnight, but

Marcello does not let go of my hand. Instead, he takes my other hand in his as well. We look each other in the eyes. I want so much for him to kiss me, to take me in his arms, and hold me. Yet, as he bends his head toward mine, our lips just about to touch, I step back and let go of his hands.

"Marcello, I am truly sorry. I like you very much. You are so kind, easy to talk to, and I enjoy being with you more than I can explain, but I am only here for another month. I must return to America. I have family, a home, responsibilities. I cannot start a relationship with a man in Italy. Please forgive me."

"It was simply a goodnight kiss, Glenda. I was not expecting more. I do understand your concern. It is OK. Please forgive me if I overstepped." Marcello turns and walks away. I stand there watching him go, a lump in my throat and tears stinging my eyes.

Chapter Eleven

I AM DEPRESSED WHEN I GO TO BED. THROUGHOUT THE night I toss and turn, waking frequently and thinking of Marcello. Finally, falling into a deeper sleep sometime after four, I sleep until nine, which is late for me. My body feels tired and sore as I do my morning exercise, shower, and get dressed. In my mind, I go over yesterday again and again. *Should I have said something the first time he took my hand? Had I misled him by holding hands during the day? Should I continue to see him? Can I trust myself to be with him? I like him so much. Will he be at the bar? Will he really still want to see me?*

It is close to ten thirty when I head out for the day. I decide I will go to the bar as usual for my coffee and see what happens. As I near the top of the hill, I look over at the bar. Sitting at the table is Marcello, but he is not alone. There is another woman sitting with him. I do not recognize this woman. *Who is she? Is this someone he already knows, or did he just meet her today?* They appear to be enjoying their conversation. *What do I do? Should I go sit inside the bar? Should I go say "Good morning," waiting to be invited to join them?*

Deciding I will not be pleasant company today, I turn away from the bar and walk down the main road toward Marcena. Soon Giorgio comes driving up the road. He beeps his horn, pulling over to talk to me. "What are you doing for lunch today, Glenda?"

"Nothing in particular."

"Wanda says come have lunch at the house. You want to come?"

"OK, that would be very nice. I will go on my walk first, then meet you at your house later."

"OK, ciao, ciao."

I walk down to the lumberyard, where I stand listening to the rush of the water in the river for a minute. Then I go up the road past Vecchia Segheria, continuing until I reach a camping area. Turning right, I stroll along the dirt road until I am near Mocenigo.

Still too early for lunch, I turn left and go up the road to the edge of the mountain. I walk along a path where there are several wood carvings made from stumps of fallen trees. I take time to admire each unique carving: an eagle in flight, an old man, a mamma bear and her cub, a wolf, an owl, and an eagle protecting a bunny rabbit. Here I pick up the path Ziro del Lez, which takes me to Lanza. On the way through Lanza, I stop at the cemetery to commune with the ancestors. I arrive at Giorgio and Wanda's just in time for lunch.

Wanda has once again made a fabulous meal: cheese, salami, pasta, baked chicken, salad, fresh strawberries over gelato, wine, coffee. I feel truly blessed to be in their home—to be able to call them my friends. During the meal, I feel Giorgio and Wanda watching me. I can sense a conversation going on between them when they look at each other. Couples who have been together a long time have a way of looking at each other and knowing what the other is thinking.

Wanda says something I cannot interpret. Giorgio shakes his head and asks, "Glenda, are you OK? Wanda is worried about you. You are not the happy, laughing, funny person we know. You are not talking much. That is a bad sign. Do you feel OK?"

Giorgio and Wanda have become some of my best friends in the world, certainly my best friends in Italy. Surely I can talk to them about anything. I take a deep breath. "I am sad, and confused. You know about the man I met. He has been kind to me, showing me special places here in Val di Non. His name is Marcello."

"Yes, you are always teasing that you want a man. You said you need to find a man so you can get married and live in Italy. Now you have one. It is perfect, yes?"

"I know I often say I am looking for a boyfriend. I ask about different men in town. I joke about needing a husband to keep me warm so I can live here in the winter. You know I am teasing. I don't expect to really find a man."

"Yes, but if you have one, there is no problem. Get married, stay warm, live in Italy."

Deep sigh. "Well, last night he tried to kiss me goodnight, but I moved away and would not kiss him. Now, maybe he does not even want to be friends. I don't know what to do."

"Oh no, this is not a conversation for a man. This is only for women to talk about. I must leave."

"NO, Giorgio. You must interpret for me. Wanda is my friend. She is my advisor. She needs to help me. Sit down and interpret for me. You don't have to give your opinion, simply interpret."

Reluctantly, Giorgio sits down, sharing with Wanda what we have discussed. They both start chuckling.

"You are laughing at me! My life is in turmoil and you are laughing!"

"You are funny, Glenda. You are like all women. You say you want something, then when you get it, you don't want it. Crazy." Interpreting for Wanda, "What did Marcello say when you did not kiss him?"

"I explained that I like him very much, but I am here for about another month. Then I must return to America where I have family and responsibilities. He said he understood, then he turned around and walked away."

"Do you think he does not want to be your friend anymore?"

"Oh, I don't know. The problem is I really like him. I wanted him to kiss me. I wanted to kiss him back. How can I want that when I must leave soon? I must be OK with being friends. I do not want to have a fling."

"A *fling*? What is a *fling*? I do not know how to interpret it."

"A *fling* is an affair. It is usually a short relationship that results in casual sex but does not result in a long-lasting solid relationship. I don't want to kiss him once or twice, have sex one night, and then go back to America."

Giorgio puts his head in his hands and moans. "I do not want to have this conversation. Women are crazy." Then he goes on to interpret to Wanda what I said.

Wanda asks, "You have not seen him today?"

"No, I wanted to talk to him. When I walked up the hill, I saw him at the bar. He was sitting at MY table. You know I have a table at Bar Lanterna I always sit at. It is my table. He was sitting there with a woman. They were talking and laughing. I could not go talk to him about last night with another woman sitting there, so I went for my walk."

"Well, Glenda. I think you need to listen to your heart. Relationships are a lot of work. They are not easy to maintain, but you must communicate. Giorgio and I were fortunate to be from the same town. We knew each other as friends for a long time before we fell in love. We have a good marriage, nonetheless it takes a lot of communicating. You do not see us when we are fighting, but believe me there are times I want to put my hands around his neck and strangle him. Men are challenging. When we both calm down, then we talk and work it out.

"I think you need to talk to Marcello. It is difficult knowing you must return to America, but many people have met while on vacation or away from home. They find solutions that work for them. If you talk, maybe together you will find a solution, or maybe you will both agree you need to remain friends. Later, if you are both unquestionably in love with each other, you will know what is best for both of you. Even friends must talk to maintain their friendship."

I nod my head, not sure what else to say. I know she is right.

"Perhaps today is not the best time to talk to him. Maybe you need a little break from thinking about him. Giorgio and I are going to visit Roland and Elfriede this afternoon. Would you like to come with us?"

"I would enjoy that. Thank you. You are a good friend, Wanda."

We have a lovely afternoon together. After having a glass of wine at Roland and Elfriede's house, they decide to take me on a little journey. We drive to a spot near Lana, park and walk up a hill. Roland assures me that it will be a simple walk, but it is a little steep for me. I am thrilled when we get to the top. There before my eyes is another amazing waterfall. My friends know how to make me happy.

Driving back into town, Giorgio drives past Bar Lanterna. Marcello is there talking with a different woman. "You want to stop, Glenda?"

"No, Giorgio. He is with another woman. I cannot talk with him with another woman there. I will try to find him at the bar tomorrow before he leaves for Torino."

Giorgio and Wanda drop me off at my apartment. I am extremely tired, having not slept well the night before. I read for a short time but can't keep my eyes open. When I lie down, I fall right to sleep; nonetheless, I wake several times during the night. I get up at seven feeling like I have not slept at all. I dress and head for the bar. I hope that I will find Marcello there having coffee before he heads to Torino. Marcello is not outside at the table, so I go inside hoping to find him there.

Donatella looks surprised to see me when I enter. "You are very early, Glenda."

"Yes, I did not sleep well, so I came to have an early breakfast."

Donatella notices me scanning the bar. "Marcello was already here. He said he had to return to Torino early today." I shake my head. "He was here many hours yesterday. I think he was waiting for you. He came again in the evening and waited a long time."

"Oh, I had lunch with Giorgio and Wanda. Then we went to Val d'Ultimo to visit some friends. I had not told Marcello. I don't have his cell phone number, so I could not message him to tell him."

Donatella squints her eyes and has an expression on her face that makes me think she doesn't understand what I said. Then her face brightens. "I think he will be back."

"Maybe." I go outside to drink my coffee and eat my

pastry. I decide to go home, skipping my walk for the day. I will sit in my garden, read, and work crossword puzzles. It is going to be a long day.

Chapter Twelve

THE NEXT DAY I FEEL BETTER. I HAD SLEPT WELL, having been so exhausted. I had also rationalized that although I should have gone to the bar to talk to Marcello, there was nothing I could do about it now. *I don't have his phone number or a way to reach him.* I also rationalized that I had not done anything wrong. *I told him I liked him. I was honest with him about why I felt I could not have a relationship beyond friends.* If he didn't like that and wanted to play the field, then so be it. If he returns before I leave, I will take Wanda's advice and talk with him. If he does not return, then maybe it is not meant to be. I need to get back into my routine.

I have my usual morning coffee followed by my walk, relax a bit, and have lunch. In the afternoon, I drive to Cles to do some shopping. When I return, I find a note on my doorstep. It is from Romina and Roberta. It says they are the daughters of Bruno, the son of Natalia Bacca. They have come before to meet me, but I was not here. They are trying again to find me and are eager to meet. Can I please call them when I return?

I am delighted beyond belief. *More family to meet!* I take time to put away my groceries. As I pick up my phone to call them, the doorbell rings. Standing before me are three strangers, two women and a man. It must be my new family.

Romina and Roberta both speak English, so they interpret for their father. They can only stay a few minutes. We make arrangements for me to visit them at their home for lunch later in the week.

The following day, I have once again been invited to Giorgio and Wanda's for lunch. It is a dark, dreary day. We are predicted to have thundershowers for the next three days. During our marvelous meal, it begins to rain. We can hear the rumble of thunder in the distance. Soon it turns into a thunderstorm much like the summer thunderstorms I remember as a child growing up in New Mexico: lightning everywhere, combined with thunder so loud it sends chills up your spine. The downpour of rain is tremendous. Water rushes down the streets from the mountains, and for a short time it hails. As the storm drives on, we sit and visit.

I pull out a little speech I have written to give at the Rotary meeting Giorgio will attend with me in a couple of weeks. Giorgio corrects my spelling along with my terrible Italian grammar. Then I practice reading my speech. Giorgio and Wanda both laugh heartily as I mispronounce every other word. I keep putting the accent on the wrong syllable, until finally Giorgio takes the paper and puts accent marks above the correct syllable of every word. We all get quite a laugh over my feeble attempt to speak Italian.

In spite of the rain, we venture out to visit Wanda's sister Carla and her family. It is a lovely visit. When the rain stops, we all pile into cars and drive to Hotel Viridis in Cagnò for gelato. What a perfect day!

A couple of days later I meet Marinella at the bar for breakfast. After breakfast we go for a short walk. "Are you going to see Marcello again before you leave?"

"I don't know. He has been coming about every two to three weeks. I should be able to see him again."

"Do you like him?"

"I like him. He is a nice friend, but I must be realistic. I live in America. It would be exceptionally difficult to have a long-distance relationship with a man in Italy."

"That is true. Besides, he lives in Torino. I do not think you would like Torino. It is a huge city."

"Another reason why it is not good to think of him as more than a friend." *Easier said than done. I cannot get Marcello out of my head. I think about him several times a day. I want so much to talk to him.* We go our separate ways after our walk, agreeing to get together in the evening for coffee.

I wake early the next day, excited. Today, I am going to Marcena to have lunch with my cousin Bruno and his family. After my usual morning routine, I take time to translate an article from one of the newspapers given to me by my cousin Luigi. At noon, I head off to Marcena.

I meet Bruno's wife, Mariagrazia, who along with Roberta and Romina have fixed a fabulous lunch: *canederli*, cabbage salad, potatoes, chicken, fruit, bread, gelato, coffee, and grappa. I especially enjoy Bruno's homemade wine! I have brought my tablet along with photos from home. They also share family photos with me and give me details about the members of Natalia Bacca's family as I take notes for my family tree. We have an enjoyable time talking.

Romina shares, "We have a lot of family living in Canada. They live in Toronto. I will give you their names, addresses, and phone numbers so you can get in touch with them too."

"Wonderful. I appreciate that."

Roberta asks, "Glenda, why did it take you this long to come to Rumo to find your family? Why didn't you come when you were younger?"

"I thought I needed to wait until I could stay for several months. At first, I thought Rumo was a very large town. I thought it would take a long time to figure out if any of the people were my family. I did not realize I was related to half the town." They find this quite amusing.

Next comes the tour of the house. From the balcony on the top floor is an attractive view of the valley. Looking straight down, you can see their large, immaculate garden with a chicken coop nearby. We go down into the cellar, which soon becomes my favorite part of the house. There is a workroom where Bruno keeps all his tools and another room that serves as a second kitchen for making preserves as well as their own salami and speck.

Finally, my favorite room of all—the cantina! This is a real cantina with four stainless steel vats for making excellent homemade wine. Hanging from the ceiling to cure are salami and speck. I can see myself visiting cousin Bruno frequently for a late afternoon snack and *vino*. They are such kind people, so fun to talk to. I feel tremendously fortunate to have this day with them. It is already five before I head home.

The days are speeding by quickly. Many things happen over the next week and a half. It helps to keep my mind off Marcello. When the Friday arrives that I expect him to visit, he does not show up. I am terribly disappointed. I had hoped he would not give up on me that easily, but what can I do? Thankfully, my family and friends keep me busy.

When I had lunch at Bruno's last week, they asked if I had met Carlo, the son of Angela Bacca. When I told them no, Romina said she would take me to interpret for me when she had time. I received a text from Romina this morning saying she was available in the late afternoon. It is raining, so I drive to Marcena to pick up Romina.

It is a pleasing visit. Carlo is the oldest living relative I have in Rumo. He is kind, welcoming us into his home and offering us some tea to drink. He shows me pictures of his wife who had died in a car accident many years ago. He is clearly proud of his daughters. He wants me to meet Milva, his daughter who lives there and helps to run the gas station; however, Milva is eight months pregnant with twins and on bed restriction by doctor's order. I will have to wait to meet her another time.

Chapter Thirteen

Monday morning, I have my cappuccino with pastry as usual, but I skip my walk so I can go to Fondo to shop for some gifts. I eat a light lunch when I get home. I am debating taking a walk, or doing that after I read and practice some Italian. It surprises me when the doorbell rings. Marcello stands before me when I open the door. I hold my breath for a second. "Marcello, I assumed when you did not arrive on Friday that you would not be coming back. This is a surprise."

"A good surprise, I hope."

"Yes, would you like to come in?"

"No, I am hoping you are free to go for a walk with me."

"Certo, let me get my things."

We begin our walk by going down a road behind the apartment. This road takes us past several apple orchards and raspberry fields and on into Marcena. We walk some distance with neither of us saying anything. The silence is beginning to feel uncomfortable, when Marcello starts, "Glenda, I am sorry I made you mad the last time I was here. I did not mean to upset you or offend you."

"Oh, Marcello. I was not mad at you. I was confused."

"I wanted to talk to you. I waited for a long time at Bar Lanterna on Sunday, but you never came. I came to your apartment three times in the afternoon to see if you were home. You never answered the door. I went to the bar again in the evening. Still you did not come. I was certain you were angry with me and avoiding me."

"I am truly sorry. I started to come to the bar in the morning. When I got near the top of the hill, I saw you sitting at the table with another woman. I did not want to talk to you with another woman sitting there, so I went for my walk. Giorgio invited me to lunch, and then after lunch Giorgio and Wanda took me with them to visit our friends in Val d'Ultimo. I am sorry I did not let you know I was going with them. I do not have a phone number to contact you. When we returned, Giorgio drove past the bar and you were there with a different woman. I went home. I thought maybe you had chosen to be with these women because I had rejected you."

"Oh, Glenda. I was praying you would come rescue me from these women. I did not invite them to my table. They simply sat down and started talking. I wanted you to chase them away. I am not a gigolo! I am a patient man. I am not ready to look for another woman. Are we still friends?"

"I truly hope so. I am very attracted to you, Marcello. I like you, and I enjoy the time we are together. The problem is not you. The problem is that I cannot maintain a relationship with a man for more than a couple of months when he lives in the same town as me. How can I maintain a relationship with a man thousands of miles away?

"Also, how do I choose between the love for my family and friends in America, versus those in Italy? It is a little overwhelming. I know you said it was merely a goodnight kiss, but goodnight kisses lead to other things. I don't want to have a man for only a night or two every now and then. I want to find a man I can spend every night with for the rest of my life, which I hope is many years yet."

"I think the length of the relationship is not affected by the distance of the two people, but more by the quality of the relationship. Perhaps we need more time to get to know each other. I think we need to exchange phone numbers so we can communicate when we are not in the same town. Maybe after I retire, I can come visit you in America. I hope you will come again to Italy. With more time and opportunity to know one another, we will know if we are better as friends, or if there is more for us than that. I am a patient man, Glenda. I can wait for a goodnight kiss."

"I like your ideas, Marcello. Thank you."

"You are really attracted to me? What is it you like about me?"

"Well, you are handsome, you do not smoke, and you are funny."

"Oh yes, your criteria for a man. However, I am not rich."

"I think you are not poor either. You like wine, and you say you have a passion for cooking. I am not much of a cook, so that might make up for you not being rich." Marcello laughs heartily.

I continue, "I like your name very much. It is a sexy name. It suits you. We do have things in common. We like to travel, enjoy the mountains, and like to trek. You are a patient man. You let me ramble on and on, telling you my stories without interrupting me. You listen carefully to everything I say. Most importantly, I think you are a kind man with a soft heart."

Marcello stops walking as he turns to look at me. I say, "I watch your face as we talk. I can see the compassion in your eyes as we talk about family and friends. I think you are a man who takes good care of the people he loves."

Marcello looks at me for a minute. He suddenly turns and starts to walk again. "I think we need to walk or I might try to kiss you again!" he says. I chuckle as I walk beside him. A couple of minutes later he asks quietly, "Is it still OK for friends to hold hands, or is it better if we do not do that?" I silently slide my hand into his, and he squeezes it tightly. "I hope you had exciting adventures while I was gone. Tell me all."

I tell Marcello about meeting Bruno and his family, as well as having met Carlo.

"I cannot believe how many people in this community you are related to. I think the whole town is truly your family."

"I know. I love it! I had two spectacular trips while you were gone. First my cousin Elio took me on a wonderful trip along with his girlfriend, Luisa; Luisa's sister, Paola; and Paola's husband, Albino. We left at six and drove all around the Dolomiti mountains near Bolzano.

"First, we stopped at Lago di Carezza, a glassy lake with sea-green, crystal-clear water. The reflection of the mountain off the water was amazing! Then, we went to Val di Fassa where we went to Costalunga Pass, Sella Pass, Canazei, and Pordoi Pass. I could not believe how high up these passes went and the sharp hairpin turns as we traveled up the mountain. I could not believe the bicyclists. How can they possibly ride their bikes up these mountains? It is unbelievable.

"From there we went to the town of Ortisei to do some shopping and had coffee. Our final stop was in Bolzano. We went to the home of my cousin Giovanni, Elio's brother. I met Giovanni's wife, Rosanna, along with his daughter, Cristina. Giovanni looks a lot like my brother Jim, loving to joke and tease like him too. We had dinner together, after which we went to a bar for coffee and grappa. It was a fun visit. I hope to return to Bolzano someday to shop and see some of the historical buildings there."

"That sounds like a perfect day, Glenda. I agree with you. I am not a bicyclist either, and I can't imagine how they go up those steep mountains. Maybe someday I can go with you to Bolzano. I hear it is a lovely city. So, tell me about your other trip."

"I went on a grand excursion with my cousin Bruno and his family. This time, instead of going northeast, we went northwest. We stopped first in Tonale where we visited the World War I memorial, Monumento Ossario."

Having a sudden memory, I get excited and fling my arm out, hitting Marcello hard on the shoulder. He jumps and looks at me with wide eyes. "Oh my gosh, Marcello. You have been keeping secrets from me! It just so happened that while we were looking at the monument in Tonale, Romina said, 'Look, there's zio Claudio.' My cousin Bruno has a brother, Claudio, and his wife, Graziella, who live in Torino."

Marcello's face lights up with realization as he laughs. "Claudio is your friend who suggested you visit Rumo when you wanted to get away from Torino. He told me he had heard all about me from you. Why didn't you tell me I had a cousin in Torino?"

"Oh, Glenda, I wanted to surprise you. I had hoped he would come to Rumo some weekend when I was here. I wanted to be the one to introduce you to your family."

"That would have been nice. It was still a fabulous surprise. We did not visit for long because they were going the opposite direction as us. One day I hope to see them again.

"OK, back to my story. From Tonale we went to the town of Tirano, which is near the Italian-Switzerland border. Here we went into the most magnificent church, the Basilica della Madonna di Tirano. Its beauty took my breath away with all its marble, gold, and ornate decorations. Then we went up Passo Stelvio. I knew the passes Elio took me to were tall, but this was even bigger: thirty-six hairpin turns going to the top of the pass, and fifty coming back down. Unbelievable!

"At the bottom of the pass we stopped for a picnic lunch, and then we drove to Resia. There are three lakes, but if I understood correctly the last lake was formed when the old town flooded. The town is still buried under the water, but at one point you can see a church steeple rising out of the water. It was fascinating to see. We came home going through Merano. It was such an awesome experience, Marcello. I wish you had been with us."

"I wish I had been with you too. I would have enjoyed seeing your face when you met Claudio. It would have been a good opportunity for me to get to know your family, not to mention, it would have been an educational opportunity for me as well. There is much about this region I still do not know."

We walk for at least two hours in a large circle around Rumo. We are back in Mione walking up to the bar when Donatella greets us cheerfully. As evening comes on, we are joined by Marinella, Gianluca, and Loredana. Many people stop at the table to say hello to Marcello. Everyone is happy to see him back in town. We spend a relaxing evening going to Cles for dinner with Marinella and Gianluca.

Chapter Fourteen

I AM THRILLED THE NEXT MORNING TO BE GOING FOR breakfast at the bar with Marcello. It has been too long. He is already at the bar when I arrive. Thankfully, there is no other woman sitting at the table with him.

"Buongiorno, Glenda. I saw you coming up the hill, so I ordered your usual. Donatella will have it ready in a minute."

"Thank you. It feels a little strange having breakfast with you during the week. We never talked about why you were not able to come on Friday, or how long you will be able to stay."

"I had many important meetings at work on Friday, which kept me from getting away. Then I had a niece in Milano who graduated from the university. We had a big family celebration for her on Saturday. My brothers from Germany and Switzerland even came, which allowed me to spend Sunday with them. I actually must return tomorrow for work."

My heart sinks a little. This is going to be such a short visit. I try not to let him see my disappointment. "Did you spend all day eating like we did for Giorgio's and Roland's birthdays?"

"Yes, every celebration includes lots of food. That is the Italian way. There was music, dancing, jokes, and gifts. A big party."

Suddenly, Giorgio appears at the table. He was on his way to the apartment to find me when he saw me at the bar. I introduce Giorgio to Marcello. They shake hands as they go into a conversation, rapidly exchanging back and forth at a speed I can't interpret. "Hey, what are you talking about? Who is going to interpret for me?"

"This is man's talk, Glenda. You do not need to know what I say to your friend," Giorgio jokes, laughing at me. "Wanda sent me to find you. We had heard your friend is back in Rumo. She wants to meet Marcello. She is inviting both of you to dinner tonight. You be there at seven thirty, OK?"

I look at Marcello, and he nods his head in agreement. "OK, Giorgio. Thank you. We will be there."

"I will tell Wanda. She will be happy. Ciao, ciao."

"That is kind of your friends to invite us to dinner. We should take some wine with us. What kind of wine do they like?"

"Giorgio's favorite wine is Barolo. He also likes Teroldego. I think, however, that he will be happy with any wine we take. I do not know if Wanda has a preference."

"OK, then this afternoon we will go wine shopping."

"Always one of my favorite things to do, especially if we get to drink some as we shop. Oh, Ivano and Luisa, friends I have met through Giorgio and Wanda, live in Nogaredo. They have told me about a winery they think I should visit. It is called Grigoletti winery. Can we go try their wine this afternoon?"

"Certo, Glenda. I want to talk to you about an idea I had last night. I don't know if you will like this idea, but I hope you will say yes. You said you believe your grandmother's parents and two siblings were from Piemonte region. I have a friend who does a lot of family research in the area. If you want, you can give me the information on your family, and I will see if he can verify if they were born there."

"Then, I would like for you to come with me to Torino tomorrow when I leave. You can stay at my daughter's house, while I will be at my house. I already asked my daughter if that will be possible, and she said yes. I will have to work part of the time, but I will also be able to leave work early in order to show you around Torino.

"Maybe your cousin Claudio and Graziella can join us for dinner one night. If my friend finds information on your family, we can meet up with him also. I will bring you back to Rumo on Sunday. I know this is sudden."

My head is spinning. I am not sure if I am more excited or frightened by the idea. *It is a fabulous opportunity to get to know my cousin, meet Marcello's children, spend more time with Marcello, and see if I can find documentation on my grandmother's family. I would be crazy not to do it, right?*

"Why not! This is such a kind offer, Marcello. Thank you."

"Really? You will go with me to Torino? I expected you to say no."

"You told me the first time I met you that you are an honorable man. I can trust you. I would like to meet your children and get to know my cousin. I want to find out more about my grandmother's family, yet must have help to do it. So, why not!"

"Exactly, why not!"

"After breakfast, I will message Ivano to see if we need reservations to go to the winery and to get directions. Then we can go to my apartment, so I can get the information on my grandmother's family. Next, we can take our walk, have a little lunch, and then this afternoon we will go wine tasting and shopping. Does that sound like a fair plan?"

"Perfetto, Glenda. Perfetto."

We proceed with our plan. After giving Marcello the sketchy information on my grandmother's family, he makes a call to his friend. His friend is more than happy to see what he can find. He understands that I am only positive that they were from the Piemonte region, but not certain their birthdates nor birthplaces are correct. He is intrigued by the challenge.

While on our walk, I receive a message from Ivano. "Ivano says we do not need reservations for the winery, but he will call to let them know anyway. Giorgio will be at Ivano's this afternoon to check on his beehives he keeps on Ivano's property. Will it be OK if Ivano and Giorgio join us at the winery? Can we meet at two? Is that OK with you, Marcello?"

"Absolutely. It will be nice to spend time with your friends."

I respond that we will be happy to meet them at that time.

Following a salad lunch at the bar, we head out. Marcello had found a wine store in Trento online, so we go there first. It is a large store that carries a number of wines from all around Italy, as well as grappa, whisky, cognac, and rum. My sampling of Italian wine has been rather limited; on the other hand, Marcello seems familiar with many of the wines in stock. He finds a Barolo he thinks is exquisite and buys two, one for Ivano and one for Giorgio.

We arrive at Grigoletti's before Giorgio and Ivano. We wait outside, admiring the view. At first it appears to be a very small winery with vineyards going up the hill. Quite some distance away, there is a sign that reads "Grigoletti." On the outside of the winery is a giant wine barrel made to look like a house with a roof and a window with a flower box. The flower box is filled with light pink and fuchsia colored flowers. It is darling. On the wall of the winery is a painting of a giant grapevine with grapes hanging down. Beside the painting, there are real plants growing along the wall. There is a small patio with a table and chairs. It is such an inviting place.

Ivano and Giorgio arrive, and I introduce Marcello as we go inside. The size of the tasting room also gives the feel that the winery is small. All of their wines are displayed on one wall. They have twelve wines, both whites and reds. Some of their wines are award winning. We are greeted by Marica, who speaks English. She will be our tour guide at this family owned and operated winery.

As we begin our tour, I realize it is not as small as it had initially appeared. I am stunned as we go down in the cellars where the wine barrels and bottled wines are stored. It is absolutely spectacular. The walls along with the floors are all marble, with huge marble columns as supports. Amazing carvings adorn the walls, and statues of lions protect the wine. There is a special room with the ceiling made from wine bottles. In this room is stored a bottle of each wine produced over many years. There is also a large room with tables for special events.

I am so taken by the beauty of the place that I fail to hear anything Marica has to say about the wine itself. It is clear that this family understands quality. It is not hard to speculate that given the amount of time and patience they had in building their cellar, they definitely would take the time and care to produce a splendid product. The tasting proves me right. The wines are exceptional. Giorgio and Ivano are about to pay for some wine when Marcello steps in. "Please, allow me to pay for this wine."

"No, you cannot do that," they say in unison.

"I must. You have shown me a wonderful time in sharing this beautiful winery with me. I want to buy it, and Giorgio, you can save yours for another occasion. I am buying the wine for dinner tonight."

Giorgio smiles broadly. "Well, OK, if you must. Thank you."

I was impressed with Marcello's generosity. Leaving the building, Ivano, Giorgio, and Marcello converse in Italian. I only pick up a few words. As we get in the car, I ask Marcello, "What were you boys talking about?"

"Ivano invited us to go to Marzadro, the grappa factory, which is near his house. Then we will go by his house for coffee before we drive back to Rumo. I said yes. Is that OK?"

"Yes. Another adventure! Why not!"

Marcello laughs. "Oh, Glenda. You and your adventures, you and your wine, you and your boys. You are crazy. That is one of the things I like best about you."

Marzadro is a large, modern-looking building. We arrive in time to join a group going on a short tour. We learn that Marzadro is the family name of the people who started the business in 1949. We also learn that grappa is made by distilling pomace, the pulp that remains after the grapes have been crushed, making it a concentrated, strong alcohol. We also learn that grappa, like wine, is aged in barrels. It is all interesting; nonetheless I have tasted grappa several times, and tasting similar to vodka, it is way too strong for me. I don't think I want to taste any here.

When we get up to the tasting room, however, I find they have grappa that is flavored with herbs. In addition, they have various liqueurs in many fruit flavors. I must try the peach and pear liqueurs. Then, lo and behold, I find the

Crema Alpina Caffè, a cream liqueur mixed with coffee. Delicious enough to have as a dessert.

"Glenda, I cannot believe all the bottles you are taking home with you. How will you drink all of this before you go to America?"

"I won't. We can take some with us to Torino. Then I will give it to my friends and family. I like to give people gifts. I have to support the Italian economy. It is my home."

At Ivano's house, Marcello meets Luisa. He seems comfortable with my friends. Marcello gives Ivano and Giorgio the bottle of Borolo he bought for them. Giorgio is thrilled. "Thank you, Marcello. What a fantastic surprise. Why you do this for us?"

"To thank you. Ivano shared his community and home with me. You and Wanda have invited me to dinner tonight. I want to show my appreciation. Of course, I am hoping you will share the Borolo with me tonight."

Giorgio teases, "No, I save this for another occasion. We will drink the wine from Grigoletti tonight." They both laugh.

For a late afternoon snack, we have a little wine, salami, and cheese followed by a cup of coffee. We head back to Rumo, where the evening is relaxing and joyful. The dinner at Giorgio and Wanda's is superb. Sandro is there as well. They speak a lot of Italian. Once in a while, Giorgio or Marcello tell me what they are saying. I have the sense they are grilling Marcello about his work, family, and childhood. He does not seem to mind. I think they are fast becoming best friends.

"Oh, by the way, I am going to be gone for a few days. Tomorrow I am going with Marcello to Torino." Giorgio and Wanda's eyes almost pop out of their heads. I have to look away to keep from laughing at them. "I will return on Sunday. I will be staying at Marcello's daughter's house in Chivasso. Marcello is going to show me some of the special places in Torino. Also, he has a friend who is looking for records on my great-grandfather and great-grandmother. I hope to return with information on my grandmother's family."

"Brava, Glenda. This will be a fantastic trip for you. Marcello, I trust you will take good care of our friend. If she returns unhappy, you will have to answer to Wanda!"

"Don't worry. I promise to behave myself and ensure she enjoys her visit."

Chapter Fifteen

We leave Rumo at six on Wednesday morning. It is approximately a five-hour drive to Torino. Marcello needs to be home in time to go into work that afternoon. As rude as it seems, I cannot help but sleep the first couple of hours on the road. Too much wine the day before, staying up late visiting at Giorgio and Wanda's, and getting up early to pack a bag to be ready by six had taken a toll on me.

I like the *autostrada* in Italy. Truckers are required to stay in the right-hand lane. You can go fast. All along the autostrada are places to quickly exit for gas, food, and coffee and hop back on the road. Not that it is difficult in America, but it is more convenient in Italy. Traffic flow varies like anyplace else. During the time people are going to work, it is heavier. After that, it is not bad. As we come to Milano, the number of lanes increases, as does the number of cars and congestion. I would like to say the speed of traffic slows down, yet that is not necessarily the case. Italians seem to love to drive fast, traffic or no traffic.

We arrive in Chivasso a little before noon. I am slightly nervous about meeting Arianna, relaxing immediately after Marcello introduces us.

"Piacere, Glenda. My father has told us a little about you. I am happy you have come so we could get to know you better. I hope you feel welcomed in my home."

"Piacere, Arianna. Grazie for letting me stay with you. I hope it is not too inconvenient."

"The inconvenience will be yours. My son is incredibly active. He loves attention. He will want you to play with him all day and night. You might not get much rest here. Come in. My husband is home for lunch. I will introduce you to both of them."

As we enter the house, I can hear laughter. Father and son are obviously playing. They come running as they hear us enter. Marcello bends down as a young boy comes flying into his arms laughing.

"Glenda, this is my husband, Luca, and my son, Damiano. We call him Dami for short."

"Piacere. I am pleased to meet you, Luca. Ciao, Dami." Damiano looks at me with these great big brown eyes and clings to his grandfather as though he is afraid that I will snatch him away. Luca takes my bag to put in my room. Then we all go into the kitchen and gather around the table. We drink white wine with our antipasto, then a glass of Nebbiolo with a simple lunch of pasta and salad, followed by coffee with fruit for dessert. It is very refreshing. As we eat, we banter back and forth about my visit to Italy and my search for my family, followed by how Arianna and Luca met.

"Thank you for this delicious meal, Arianna."

"This was a simple meal. My father is the cook of the family. We are going to his house tonight where he will make us a feast."

"Ah, you said you had to get back in order to go to work, not so you can spend the afternoon cooking a dinner."

"Well, I do have to do some work. Most of it I can do with telephone calls or on the computer. So, I will be working from home where I can cook at the same time. Of course, first I must do the shopping. I better get going."

"Luca needs to return to work this afternoon. I have a friend who is willing to come stay with Dami while he naps. I would like to take you around our little town."

"I would like that, Arianna. Thank you."

Arianna and I head out for our visit around town. They live near the downtown area, allowing us to walk the short distance. Arianna shows me a picturesque cathedral as well as the small church where she and Luca were married. Arianna has the sweetest expression on her face as she reminisces about her wedding day.

As we walk along the streets, Arianna wants to find a new shirt for Luca, so we browse in the men's clothing store. We visit the local bookstore where I find an English copy of the book on award-winning Italian wineries that we had seen at Bellaveder. After exploring a couple of women's clothing stores, we head for the gelato shop. Our conversation has been focused on the things we liked in each store. As we sit to relax, Arianna focuses on more personal aspects.

"I think my father likes you very much. From the moment he met you, he has not stopped talking about you."

"That is nice to hear. I like him too. He is a kind and gentle man. I have enjoyed my time with him."

"My father struggled after my mother died. He was terribly depressed. For two years he would not go out with friends. He would not travel. He would come here for dinner only occasionally. It got a little better after I had Dami. He was so happy to have a grandson and started coming weekly to dinner. Still, he stayed to himself most of the time. I was thankful my brother still lives at home to keep an eye on him. His best friend, Claudio, did get him to go to the bar a few times. Claudio also invited him over to watch soccer matches on TV and have dinner sometimes.

"Papà has never gone out with another woman that I know about. I think every place he went reminded him of my mother, so he tried to avoid going out much. I was grateful when Claudio convinced papà that he needed to get away from Torino and start interacting with more people. Claudio told him about Rumo, offering to let papà stay in the house he owns if he would go visit. I was so sure papà would graciously decline the offer that I was shocked when he said he was going."

"Your father told me he had been married and that your mother was killed in a car accident. Other than that, he has not talked about her or the accident. I can tell it is still difficult for him to discuss."

"He was driving the car. A man's car went out of control on some ice, hitting them. My father feels he is to blame for my mother's death because he should have been able to move his car out the way faster. It is not true. Many people saw the accident. They have told him again and again he is not to blame.

"My father is the kind of man who shoulders much responsibility, always feeling he is to blame when something goes wrong. At work, at home, at church, with family, with friends, it is always the same. I hope someday he will be able to accept that accidents are called *accidents* because nobody is at fault. Sometimes bad things happen that you cannot control."

"Thank you for sharing this with me. It helps me to understand him a bit better. I understand now why it is still difficult for him to talk about the accident when it happened four years ago. I did not realize I am the first woman he has spent time with since your mother died."

"Yes, my brother and I were speechless when he started to talk about a woman that he met in Rumo. It was the first time in years that we saw a light in his eyes when talking about someone other than Dami. We sensed an air of happiness around him. He started joking and teasing in a way he had not done in a long time. We were relieved that he had met you.

"Then last week he was sad, not exactly depressed like when my mother died, but sad. I asked him two or three times if something was wrong. He said no. Then one day I asked him when he was going to see you again. That is when he told me that you are an American and will be returning home soon. He thought it was better if he did not see you again. I wanted to talk about it, but he made it clear it was not something he would discuss with me.

"I don't know what changed. Maybe being with my aunts and uncles last weekend along with their husbands and wives made him realize they all gave up something to make their lives work together. Perhaps when papà spent time with my uncles, they talked with him. I don't know. I just know he called suddenly, saying he was going to Rumo for two days—he would call me when he got back. Now, here you are."

"I thought perhaps I was not going to see your father again either. We have a good relationship. I think we both want it to be more, but I am very hesitant. I do not know how to choose between America and Italy. I have never been successful in relationships. I cannot move to Italy for a man who I feel I barely know.

"Your father and I talked a lot the past couple of days. We agreed that we will continue to communicate regularly, and we will see each other as often as we can. We will continue to get to know each other; then we will see what happens. I am not opposed to moving to Italy, but I must be certain it is the right thing to do."

"I understand. I hope for both of you that it works out. Shall we go? Dami will be awake from his nap."

When we get back to the house, I sit on the floor and start playing with some of Damiano's toys. Soon he comes over to see what I am doing. Next thing I know we are playing cars, reading books, and becoming good friends. He is a delight. The rest of the afternoon goes quickly.

Chapter Sixteen

On the way to Marcello's house, Damiano keeps saying "No, no." I don't understand why until I realize he is saying "nonno," *grandpa* in Italian. Clearly, he loves his grandfather. I can see why it would be difficult for Marcello to think of leaving Italy.

When we walk into Marcello's house, it smells heavenly. Marcello scoops Damiano into his arms as he greets Arianna and me with a kiss on each cheek. It seems strange. This is the first time he has greeted me that way. I would much rather have a big hug, or even a kiss on the lips. *How can I be so fickle, telling him one time he cannot kiss me and then the next time wanting him to kiss me? Relationships. No wonder I am not successful at them.*

"Wow, that smells amazing, Marcello. What are you cooking?"

"Well, I will tell you as we eat each course. We will start with your favorite, *spritzone*. Then a white wine, Arneis, with our antipasto of *grissini*, which are special breadsticks, a meat and cheese selection, along with *fiori di zucca ripieni*, which are stuffed zucchini blossoms.

"I do not know if you will like the zucchini blossoms because they have anchovies in them. I know you do not like anchovies; however, the anchovies are mixed with mozzarella cheese and fried in the zucchini blossom. I do not think you will taste the strong flavor of anchovies. If you do not like them after you try one, it is OK. On the meat and cheese tray, I have selected for you to try three of our best Piemonte cheeses: Castelmagno, a blue cheese; Toma, a creamier cheese; and Bra, a soft cheese. I hope you like them."

"And that is just the appetizer? Are you trying to make me fatter than I am? Are you going to do a full traditional meal with a first plate, second plate, and dessert? I will not be able to move after we eat."

"I have only made small servings of everything so we cannot overeat. It is my opportunity to share with you the best of Piemonte. The point is to enjoy a long, relaxing evening with friends as you savor the food. Claudio and Graziella are coming to join us. They will be here soon. Lorenzo is taking a shower but will be out in a moment."

"I tried to tell you, Glenda, that my father is a superb cook. He finds it relaxing. He loves to try new recipes, sometimes making his own creations. He has not cooked like this for us in a long time. I am glad he has a reason to cook for us again."

"Ciao, sorella." I turn to see an extremely handsome young man give his sister a big hug and snatch his nephew from his grandfather's arms. This has to be Lorenzo. He looks a lot like Marcello. The doorbell rings as we are introduced. Claudio and Graziella have arrived. We move to sit outside on a patio surrounded by a garden full of flowers. I feel at home here. There is much talking, laughing, teasing, eating, and drinking, like my own family dinners in America.

"This is wonderful, Marcello. I like this wine. The cheeses are all delectable. I even like the zucchini blossom." Marcello looks at me with skepticism. "Honest, I am not lying to you. The anchovies are not strong at all. OK, I am not saying they are my favorite food in the world, but I would eat one again." Everyone laughs.

"Now we are switching to a Barolo wine I think you will enjoy. For our first plate, I have made you a special pasta dish called *agnolotti del plin*. It is a pasta filled with pork. After boiling, it is sautéed in butter and sage. I think you will like it. Then, for the second plate, you will have *brasato al Barolo* served with a creamy spinach and cooked carrots. Why are you shaking your head, Glenda?"

"I am in shock. I know you said you liked to cook, but you are a chef. This is a meal you would get in a fancy restaurant. It is a good thing I am not cooking. We would be having peanut butter and jelly sandwiches! I am in awe of you, Marcello."

Marcello beams with pride. He is pleased that I am impressed with his culinary skills. I can see everyone watching us out of the corner of their eyes as we talk. Claudio raises his glass. "A toast to my friend for such a fine meal."

"It is delicious. I would prefer to eat Marcello's cooking than my own," says Graziella.

Claudio assures me, "Graziella is an excellent cook. Maybe one day you will be able to enjoy her cooking as well."

For dessert Marcello serves *panna cotta*, a custard made with cream and caramel. He tops it with fresh strawberries and blueberries. It has been such a marvelous evening that I hate for it to end. Marcello has to work in the morning. Giving me a goodbye kiss on each cheek, he informs me he will pick me up at noon the next day.

I sleep well. I do not hear anyone stirring in the

morning, but I slept later than usual, so no doubt they are up. It is nine by the time I shower and dress for the day. I am greeted by Arianna and Damiano as I enter the kitchen. Luca has already gone to work. I eat only yogurt and coffee for breakfast, still being full from the dinner last night.

"You were pleased with my father's meal last night?"

"Oh yes, it was incredible. I can do more than peanut butter and jelly sandwiches, but I am not a chef. I am an average cook. I have one or two things I can cook that are special and exceptionally tasty. My mother taught me to make homemade ravioli. It is a recipe that was passed on to her by one of my Italian aunts. I had an uncle who often made polenta with a rabbit stew over it. So, my mother learned to make polenta; however, she usually put a marinara sauce on it.

"I found a recipe for 'Three Cheese Polenta.' It is layered like lasagna with a three-cheese mixture between the polenta layers. I serve it with a mushroom sauce. My family loves it. Your father, however, is obviously exceptionally skilled in the kitchen."

"Yes. He does not always cook such a big meal. Our daily meals are usually much smaller and lighter than that. He wanted to please you. I think he did a nice job. I saw how you looked at him all night. There was a special gleam in your eyes. I also noticed the gentle teasing you two did and the occasional brushing of hands."

I chuckle as I blush. "I told you I like your father very much. I would like to have more than a friendship with him. Time will tell. I did not mean to behave like a young schoolgirl making goo-goo eyes at him and flirting with him. How embarrassing!"

"Well, if it makes you feel any better, he looked at you the same way. It is interesting seeing this side of my father. I know he loved my mother, but naturally I was not around when they were young and falling in love. It is fun to watch my father act like a schoolboy. Do not get serious too fast. I enjoy seeing him try to woo you and flirt with you. It will give me something to tease him about when he is old!"

The morning continues with pleasing conversation. It is relaxing visiting with Arianna, playing with Damiano, and walking with them to the park to play. Marcello arrives exactly at noon. After a quick little lunch, we meet Claudio in the heart of Torino for a tour.

Claudio greets me with a kiss on each cheek, "Ciao, Glenda. Welcome to Torino. I am pleased you have come to visit us here. I hope you enjoy the little tour today. We are in the old historical area of Torino. I have many places to show you today."

"Grazie, Claudio, for taking the time to show me around your town. This is so kind of you. I am eager to learn about Torino. Lead the way!"

First, we walk past the Porta Palatina, the old city gate built during the Roman period. It had served as the entrance into the city. The center is filled with many ancient buildings full of rich history. We see the Palazzo Madama, Palazzo Reale (Royal Palace of Torino), and Palazzo Carignano. Next, we visit the Egyptian Museum, spending a couple of hours strolling from floor to floor looking at the artifacts.

"Glenda, I am sorry but I am going to have to leave you and Marcello," says Claudio. "Graziella is expecting me. I will see you again tomorrow, and we will spend most of the day together, OK?"

"Thank you, Claudio, for this wonderful day. I look forward to seeing you again tomorrow."

Marcello and I then go to the National Museum of Cinema. The museum is housed in a building called the Mole Antonelliana, a nineteenth-century building that serves as a major landmark and architectural symbol for the city. At the top of the building is a tall tower. We travel up the glass elevator to the top where we have a stunning 360-degree view of the city. What a fun-filled day this has been. We finish the day off by Marcello taking me to dinner at his favorite restaurant.

"Did you enjoy today, Glenda?"

"Yes, very much, thank you. I am embarrassed to say that I do not retain history well. You and Claudio shared so much with me today. I will never be able to remember all the history, but I will remember the experience."

"We would never expect you to remember our history, although we do enjoy sharing it with others. I hope you have an equally enjoyable day tomorrow."

Chapter Seventeen

Friday, Marcello has to work only for a couple of hours. We meet with Claudio, piling into his car as he will be our chauffeur for the day. We start our day at the Palazzina di caccia di Stupinigi. The Royal Hunting Lodge, located in Stupinigi, was built in the beginning of the eighteenth-century. This is a huge palace full of paintings, sculptures, antiques, and history.

After our tour through the palace, we have a bite to eat at a nearby restaurant. As we eat, I inquire, "Claudio, how did you end up here in Torino instead of Rumo?"

"When I was young, I was in the carabinieri. I was stationed here in Torino, where I met Graziella. When I left the service, I had fallen in love with Graziella, and since her home was here, I remained in the area."

"How sweet."

Marcello chimed in, "See, Glenda, I told you all the women are in charge in Italy. There would be no marriages in Italy if the men did not go where the woman wants!"

Laughing, I ask, "Do you and Graziella have children, Claudio?"

"Yes, we have a son, Andrea, and a daughter, Erica. Our son is married. He and his wife are expecting a baby soon."

"Very nice. I hope I can meet them sometime."

After lunch our next stop is the Museo Nazionale dell'Automobile, the National Automobile Museum. Marcello is like a kid in a candy store. He loves his automobiles and is thrilled to share his knowledge of the history with me. I have never been a car buff; nevertheless, I do find the museum interesting. Over two hundred cars representing various countries are spread out on three different floors of the building. There are some unusual cars and splendid displays. I am glad we visit this museum.

From the museum, we go to see two churches. The first is on top of a hill that overlooks the city. You can see the Po River, which runs through Torino. Then, on to our final stop at Basilica di Superga, which was built in the 1700s. It also sits on a hill well above the city.

"Wow, Claudio, this is a beautiful church; the view of the city from so high up is breathtaking."

"Yes, it is a lovely church but with a sad history attached to it. In May 1949, a plane carrying players of the Grande Torino soccer team crashed into the Basilica di Superga embankment. Thirty-one people died, eighteen of them members of the soccer team. There is a memorial to those who died in the crash outside the church. Shall we go see it?"

The sadness in reading the memorials does not diminish the beauty of the church or the joy of the day. Claudio and Marcello joke throughout the day, keeping me shaking my head and chuckling at the two of them. I am thankful I have the opportunity to get to know my cousin better. I am also grateful that Claudio is driving. The traffic as well as the roads in this town are crazy, with many roundabouts and cars speeding in all directions. I would be a nervous wreck trying to drive here. We go to Claudio's house to have a glass of wine with Graziella, followed by a delectable dinner at a local restaurant.

Saturday, Marcello joins us for breakfast at Arianna's house. He has brought some fresh pastries from the bakery. Arianna has yogurt, fresh fruit, and cereals for us to enjoy. Damiano is happy to sit on his grandfather's lap to eat his breakfast. Luca and Lorenzo are also here having the day off from work.

"Well, Glenda, has my father-in-law shown you the best of Torino?' I recap for Luca the places we visited. "I had no doubt he would take you to the Automobile Museum. It is his favorite place to visit. I think Dami will know more about cars when he is five than I know today."

"Yes, Marcello was especially happy there and was an informative tour guide."

Arianna chimed in, "So what is the plan for today?"

I look at Marcello because I have no idea. "Well, I have spectacular news. My friend, Pietro, has found information about your great-grandparents. We will start our day by visiting San Maurizio Canavese and Leini. Then, I will take you wine tasting—your favorite thing to do."

"Seriously, your friend found information on my family! I can't believe it. How exciting!"

Arianna laughs, "Glenda, your face is so full of joy. You do not even know what information he has."

Marcello teases, "That is Glenda. She has this thing for dead family members. That is how you know she is American. Here we would not think about them. Who cares, they are dead."

"That is not true Marcello. Italians know more about history, including the people who lived and died for this country, than any group of people I know. You don't have to go hunting for your ancestors. They are right here."

Lorenzo was on my side. "I agree, Glenda. I think it is wonderful that you want to know your ancestors. Searching for your grandfather's ancestors brought you to Rumo, where I understand you have met many family members. Maybe it will do the same for you here in Piemonte. Maybe it will bring you to Piemonte more often."

I smile. "Exactly. Why not! You never know."

Luca chimes in, "Glenda, I know we talked about your family in Rumo. Marcello also mentioned a little about your grandfather as well as your father. He never said if you have family in America. Do you have brothers and sisters?"

"Yes, I have three brothers and three sisters—seven children total in my family. I am next to the youngest. I have twenty-three nieces and nephews, along with twenty-nine great-nieces and nephews. Of course, I have aunts, uncles, and cousins. They are spread out all over the United States."

When I look up, they are all staring at me with mouths open and eyes wide. Marcello blinks and says, "Glenda, are you serious? You have all that family in America?"

"What can I say. We are a family that loves family."

We finish our breakfast and head off on our journey. The drive to San Maurizio is relaxing. Everything is a luscious green, and the air smells fresh. It is only about a forty-minute drive. My excitement mounts as we drive into the town. It is a small town of about ten thousand residents. We park on a main street near the church. Pietro is waiting for us outside the church when we arrive. Pietro only speaks Italian, so Marcello interprets for me.

"Piacere, Glenda. Welcome to San Maurizio Canavese."

"Piacere, Pietro. Thank you for helping me. I am anxious to hear what you have found out about my grandmother's family."

"Let's go inside to the church records so I can show you what I found, and I will tell you what I learned." My heart is beating fast from the excitement. I wish that I spoke Italian so I can understand everything he is saying. "OK, give me a few minutes to pull out the books that I want to share with you.

"Here we go. First, let me tell you that your great-grandfather was in fact born here in San Maurizio. You were correct that he was born in January 1853. You said his name was Giuseppe. His full name was actually Giacinto Giuseppe Aimo. Here is the record of his baptism." He opens a record book to the page documenting my great-grandfather's baptism. "You may take a photo of it if you wish, but please do not use flash."

I am speechless! My eyes are misty. Searching for my grandfather Bacca's family had been difficult, yet searching for my grandmother's family had been almost impossible. I had no real contact with anybody on my grandmother's side of the family until recently. It seems as though the family has not stayed well connected. *I cannot believe that in my first visit to Piemonte I am able to document my great-grandfather's birth.*

"I have traced your great-grandfather's family back as far as I could. I did not pull all the books with these records. I have another meeting this morning so don't have a lot of time. Perhaps another time you can come take pictures of the documents.

"I have written out for you what I found. Your great-grandfather was the son of Pietro Giuseppe, who was the son of Francesco Michele, who was the son of Giuseppe, who was the son of Francesco. I know it is confusing because names were used over and over again." Pietro goes over every descendent and who he married. I cannot believe he has written it all out for me.

"You will see that the spelling of the surname changed over time. At first it was Aymo, then Ajmo, and finally Aimo. I also have for you a copy of an article that I believe to be a link to your family. An Aimo is mentioned for the role he played in the building of an important bridge along the old Roman road Gallie in Valle d'Aosta. The article is in Italian, but Marcello can help translate it for you."

"I am amazed and speechless, Pietro. Thank you so much. I am grateful you did all of this for me."

"Oh, we are not finished. Your great-grandfather had sixteen brothers and sisters. Several of them died when they were young, but many survived. It is likely you have family living here today. Aimo is a common surname in San Maurizio. However, I did not have time to search all of these names to see who living in San Maurizio today might be a relative. You will need to return sometime if you want to do this kind of research."

"Sixteen brothers and sisters! With that many, I must have family here." Marcello and Pietro laugh at my expression. They seem to be enjoying watching my eyes grow big and the shock on my face as Pietro shares his information.

"Well, birth control was not an easy thing back then. There were often many children in a family. Speaking of family, I have more for you. You were correct on your great-grandmother's name. In this book is the documentation of the marriage of your great-grandparents here in San Maurizio. You may take a photo if you wish."

"Was my great-grandmother born here in San Maurizio, then?"

"I did not find a baptism record for her here. You had indicated that you believed she was born in Leini, but I did not have time to go there to search the records. The church office is open today until noon. If you go from here, they will help you search the records. Also, you gave me the name of a daughter, Anna, along with her birthdate. I was not able to find anything in the records here on a daughter. Perhaps her records would also be in Leini.

"In this book, though, I did find record of the son you mentioned. The birthdate you had was correct. He was baptized as Pietro Paolo Aimo. OK, let's go downstairs to the office where they will make for you an official certificate of birth for your great-grandfather together with a certificate of marriage for your records."

"Oh, Pietro. Thank you again. Please let me pay you in some way for your time and trouble."

"No, Glenda, that is not necessary. A small contribution box is in the church office. You can leave a little something there. For me, it is enough to see the pleasure on your face, knowing that you are happy with this discovery."

We obtain the documents from the church office and say goodbye to Pietro. As we walk to the car, Marcello takes my hand. I squeeze his tightly. "I am extremely thankful, Marcello. I do not know how to express how happy and grateful I am."

"As Pietro said, to see the expressions on your face is worth it. You have such an expressive face. I know when you are happy, sad, worried, puzzled. It is all there in your eyes. Would you like to go to Leini now to see if we can find your great-grandmother's baptism record?"

"What do my eyes tell you?" Marcello laughs as we get in the car and head to Leini. It is a twenty-minute drive. The town has a population of approximately sixteen thousand residents, yet does not seem to be much bigger in size than San Maurizio. We find the church with no difficulty. It does not take us long at all to find the baptism record for my great-grandmother. Instead of taking a photo of it, the office secretary makes a photocopy of the original record. She also completes a formal certificate of birth, which is signed by the priest.

Sadly, we find no record of the oldest daughter, Anna. I wonder if Anna is a middle name, not her first, but we look at records the year before in addition to the year after the birthdate I have for her. We check every Anna and every Aimo regardless of the first name. Nothing. I am satisfied with what we have.

"Now, for your next surprise. Relax because we are going to drive for about an hour and thirty minutes."

My sense of direction tells me that we head south, or maybe southwest. It is a peaceful drive. Green rolling hills, grape vineyards everywhere, flowers, and sunshine. Marcello and I talk a little about the sights, and family, but mostly we admire the view. Finally, we start going up this little hill where suddenly I see the sign: "Barolo."

"You are taking me to the town of Barolo! I didn't even know there was a town named Barolo. I thought that was just the name of the wine."

"I am confident you will like it here," says Marcello. "It is a charming little town. We will have lunch, drink some wine, and buy some wine for dinner tonight."

"I will buy some wine for my friends Giorgio and Wanda. That will make Giorgio very happy."

"Of course, you must. You cannot show up tomorrow telling him you came here but have nothing for him. I think he would double your rent payment!"

It is a joyful afternoon. We go into many different shops. Not only do I buy some Barolo for my friends, I also find some perfect gifts to take back to family in the United States. That is a reminder that I will be going home soon. As sad as that is, I am delighted to have gifts to take with me.

The drive back to Chivasso goes fast, in part because I sleep during most of it. Marcello teases me about snoring so loud it scares him and he almost drives off the road. Lorenzo meets us at Arianna's house for dinner. Marcello plays with Damiano while I share with the others the experiences that we had that day. A nice simple dinner with Barolo wine was the perfect ending to a perfect day.

Sunday, Marcello arrives for breakfast at eight. We take Damiano to the park to play for about an hour, giving Arianna and Luca some alone time. By ten, we are back at the house, ready to return to Rumo by ten thirty. I thank Arianna and Luca for their hospitality. Damiano puts his arms around my neck, giving me a goodbye kiss on my cheek. He is so sweet.

Chapter Eighteen

THE DRIVE BACK TO RUMO IS UNEVENTFUL. WE ARRIVE in late afternoon, and Marcello drops me off at my apartment so I can unpack. I message Giorgio to let him know we made it back. Giorgio and Wanda had invited us to dinner when we returned from Torino because they want to hear all about the trip. I confirm the dinner plans with Giorgio. He wants to meet at six for a *spritzone*, and I agree. I message Marcello to let him know to meet Giorgio and me at Bar Podetti at six. Then I message Marinella to see if she is around. Shortly afterward, I am at Bar Lanterna having tea with Marinella, sharing with her the documents and information I found on my family.

Dinner with Giorgio, Wanda, Sandro, and Laura is fun. Giorgio is pleased we had thought of him and brought him a bottle of Barolo. He is even happier when Marcello tells him he does not have to open it tonight; he can save it for later. I give Wanda a special bottle of olive oil. They have so many questions about the trip that I can hardly answer one question before someone asks another. It is an evening to remember.

"Thank you, my friends, for such a lovely evening and a delicious dinner. I am fortunate you take such good care of me."

"Yes," Marcello interjects in Italian. "Thank you for

inviting me to your home again. It has been a pleasure meeting you all."

Giorgio asks, "You rode here in my car from Bar Podetti. Do you want me to drive you home?"

I look at Marcello. "No," he replies. "We will walk. I will keep her safe, I promise."

As we walk, Marcello seems exceptionally quiet this evening. *I wonder if there is something specific on his mind or if he is just tired from the drive.* As we approach my apartment, he speaks up.

"Glenda, I have not wanted to tell you this. I should have said something sooner, but I did not want to spoil your visit in Torino. I must return home tomorrow morning. I will not be able to come to Rumo again before you leave for America."

My heart sinks. Somehow, I had known he was going to say this. I have been dreading this moment. I squeeze his hand. "I understand Marcello. You have responsibilities."

In front of the apartment, we stop; he turns to stand directly in front of me. He takes my other hand. "I have your phone number now. We will message each other, and sometimes we will call, right? I do not retire until the end of November. Maybe in the new year I can come visit America. Perhaps you will return to Rumo in the spring. This is not goodbye, only goodnight."

"Certo, Marcello. We will stay in contact. I am not worried. I will see you again."

He smiles. Dropping one hand, he brushes the hair off of my face, caressing my cheek with his fingers. He looks directly into my eyes. It is all I can do to keep from crying. He takes a deep breath. "Glenda, may I kiss you goodnight?"

I nod. He takes a step forward, gradually lowering his

head until our lips meet. His lips are soft and gentle on mine. Our lips part. He lifts his head, kisses my forehead, and whispers "Goodnight." He then steps back, turns, and walks away. Within seconds tears are rolling down my cheeks. I brush them away so I can see to unlock the door. The lump in my throat and ache in my chest make it hard to breathe. It is the first night in many years that I cry myself to sleep.

The last ten days of my stay in Rumo go quickly. I walk my favorite paths around Rumo. Every day, I have lunch or dinner with some member of my family. Donatella has become a close friend. One day, she takes time away from the bar to invite me to lunch with her family at her sister Paola's house. Her brother-in-law, Albino, makes *tortei di patate,* a fried potato that is a cross between hash browns and the potato pancakes my mother used to make. They are one of my favorite dishes. It is so kind and thoughtful of Donatella and her family to host me for a lunch. I have a great time.

My final dinner with my Bacca family is held in a small town about forty minutes southeast of Rumo. Giovanni and his family have come from Bolzano. Elio, Luisa, Anita, and Mario bring me with them from Rumo. Finally, I meet Franca and her husband, Franco, as well as their two children, Nadia and Stefano. Nadia speaks excellent English and serves as my translator. I have always believed that my sister JoAnn and brother Bill resemble my mother's family. Nonetheless, I can see a resemblance between them and our cousin Franca. It is a festive night filled with laughter, teasing, and the sharing of family stories.

My main purpose for my trip to Rumo was to find and meet family. I have succeeded far beyond my expectations. However, Giorgio knows that I also want to see the church records in order to get documentation of my grandfather's birth. One day, we go to the church. I am able to take a picture of the records for my grandfather, all of his siblings, and the marriage of my great-grandfather Giovanni to his wife, Cattarina. We also find a record of my great-grandfather Giovanni's death. I obtain an official document certifying my grandfather's birth.

Another day, I go on a final hike with my crazy boys—Giorgio, Roland, Ivano, and Alessio. We travel to Mount Chiodo in Val d'Ultimo, where we park by a beautiful lake. Giorgio walks with me on a road, while the others hike up the side of the mountain. We stop at a place called Fiechter Alm. When the others arrive, we have a filling lunch with another of my favorite dishes, *spezzatino*, a beef stew served over polenta.

When we leave, we all walk along the road for a bit. Then we venture off onto a little path. Shortly after, the boys leave the path to go gather pine cones for Alessio's wife, Liliana. I follow them over to where Alessio is climbing the trees like a monkey and pulling down pine cones.

As we head back down the mountain, we come to a point where there is a big step from one level of dirt to the next. I hesitate, as there is a stream with mud all around it. Sure enough, when I step down, I slip in the mud and land flat on my back. Giorgio almost has a heart attack. I am laughing so hard I cannot get up. My boys come to my rescue, but I know they will never let me forget it!

That same evening, I have a special dinner with Giorgio, Wanda, Sandro, Laura, and some of our cherished friends at Agritur Mirella. This is a quaint restaurant right by my apartment. It specializes in typical northern Italian dishes. My favorites tonight are the potato gnocchi and *strangolapreti*, which is similar to a dumpling made with bread and spinach. After it is boiled, it is sautéed in butter and sage. A superb meal to end my visit in Rumo.

Since the day Marcello left me in Rumo, he messages me every morning with a sticker that says "Buongiorno," and again every evening with one that says "Buonanotte." He calls me the day before I am to leave Rumo, and we talk for two hours. We share with each other what we have done during the week. When it comes time to say goodbye, I choke up and whisper, "I'll talk to you again soon."

It is Tuesday, July 14th. Giorgio and Wanda are taking me to the airport in Verona. For the most part it is a quiet drive. Giorgio asks, "Glenda, are you content with your visit to our area?"

"Oh, Giorgio, I am very content, truly satisfied. You all have made me enormously happy. The people in Rumo are exceptionally sweet, loving, and generous. I cannot believe I met so many family members. I love Rumo!"

"You will come back to see us?"

"Absolutely. I want to return next year in the summer instead of the spring. I want to celebrate my birthday with my Italian family and friends."

"What about Marcello? Are you sorry you are leaving him?"

"I am sorry to be leaving everyone, but I do have a nice friendship with Marcello, and I am sad to go. We will stay in touch. Who knows what will happen?"

"We will stay in touch too, Glenda. You let me know exactly when you decide to return. The summer is very busy. As soon as you decide, tell me so I can book the apartment for you."

We arrive in plenty of time, going through the line quickly to check my bags and get my boarding passes. We have a farewell glass of white wine. I give both Giorgio and Wanda a tight hug, thanking them again for their generosity.

The flight home is long but uneventful. I stop for a visit in Virginia with a nephew and his wife who have recently had their first baby. I spend five wonderful days holding and loving on this tiny little boy. I love babies. Arriving back in Turlock, it is typical summer weather: hot, hot, hot!

I message all my family and friends in Italy to let them know I have made it home safely, providing them my American phone number so we can keep in touch. Marcello continues his pattern of messaging me "Buongiorno" and "Buonanotte" every day. Sometimes he adds a message about something he has done. Other times he exchanges the sticker with a photo of a place he has visited.

I hear regularly from Giorgio as well as from Marinella. They send me updates of what is happening in Rumo. Apparently, there are many *festas* during the summer that I am missing. Of course, Giorgio and the friends continue taking hikes all summer. I receive many photos of extraordinary panoramas from their journeys.

The days fly by. I spend several days doing a deep cleaning of my house, followed by several more days working in my yard to get my garden back in shape. I visit my brothers in Turlock, sharing with them all about the family I had met.

For weeks, I meet with friends for lunches and dinners, reliving the details of my days in Italy. I try to downplay my feelings for Marcello, but some of my closest friends together with my family see through it. They say it is clear from the look on my face and shine in my eyes that I love him. Why in the world did I come back!

I give them a million reasons: my age, the logistics of moving to Italy, my house, my history of bad relationships, my family and friends here. They all shake their heads at me.

In August, I celebrate my birthday with many wishes coming from Italy. Marcello is not a fan of social media, but he hears through the grapevine that it is my birthday and video calls. The video reception is not the best, so he calls again the next day. It then becomes a weekly event for him to call me or me to call him. I look forward to those calls. Every time I go to dinner, I send him a photo along with the names of who I am with so he will have a reference when we talk.

In September, I plan a wine party with a couple of my friends to be held in my backyard at the end of October. Of course, that means going wine tasting to several different wineries as we decide what wine to have at the party. We also go shopping for little gifts to give out as we play some games. Naturally, I take pictures of all the wines we drink at the wineries we visit, sending them to Marcello as well as Giorgio and Wanda. By mid-September, Marcello and I are calling each other two to three times a week. It is making me miss him more.

In October, I start planning trips to see my family outside of Turlock: Christmas in West Virginia with my brother, February in New Mexico with my sister, March in Oregon with my nieces. By mid-October, Marcello and I are talking every day. He still messages his good morning and goodnight stickers, but he says he also needs to hear my voice. Marcello will be retiring in November and tells me about a retirement party his kids want to have for him. It sounds like fun. I wish I could be there.

It is the end of November, and tomorrow is Thanksgiving. I will be celebrating at the house of my brother Bill. I have already made a pumpkin pie, and in the morning I will make a squash casserole. I have been working on a digital family tree since I got home with all the information I gathered in Italy. I am including pictures, if I have them, of all the family. It takes a long time to put it together.

I copy the tree to DVDs to give to my family here for Christmas, as well as to send copies to Italy. I am trying to get the copies ready to be mailed to Italy today or immediately after Thanksgiving. I have no idea how long it will take for them to arrive. As I work on this project, memories of Rumo, Val di Non, family, and friends play in my head all day long. My heart is filled with gratitude and love for all the amazing people in my life.

Thanksgiving morning, I wake feeling restless and anxious. I close my eyes for a moment. Visions start coming to the surface. I feel a calmness, clarity, and certainty that I have not felt for some time. I roll over, grab my phone, and unplug it quickly from the charger. I sit up in bed and place the call.

Marcello answers, "Glenda, it is very early in the morning there. Why are you calling me? Is everything OK?"

"Marcello, I cannot get Rumo out of my head. I think about it every day. Last night I dreamt all night long. I dreamt of Rumo and the majestic trees. I dreamt of Val di Non, of the waterfalls, the canyons, the lakes, and the castles. I dreamt of family and friends. Marcello, Rumo is calling to me, I must come. I am positive that Rumo is where I belong."

"That is fantastic news, Glenda. I am happy to hear this."

"But Marcello, in every dream I had, you were there with me, standing next to me. I do not want to be in Rumo without you. Please, will you consider coming to Rumo with me?"

"Certo, Glenda. I have been waiting for you to decide if you want me in your life. I will go wherever you want me if you will have me with you. When will you come to Rumo?"

"I don't know. First, I must go see all my family to tell them goodbye and make sure they know I love them very much. Then I must do the paperwork to get permission to live in Italy, sell my house, and decide what to do with all of my property."

"Calma, Glenda, calma. Keep calm. I will help you. If you will permit me, I would like to come to America. I want to meet all of your family, and I will help you with the paperwork for Italy. I can help you pack your things. I want you to bring anything to Rumo you want, anything that will help you feel at home here in Italy. I will help you with the cost of shipping."

"Seriously, Marcello? You will do all of that for me?"

"Certo. Ti amo, Glenda. Ti amo tanto."

Tears fill my eyes. "Ti amo, Marcello. Ti amo con tutto il mio cuore."

The End

Author's Note

THIS STORY IS BASED ON THE ACTUAL SEARCH FOR MY family and my subsequent visits to Rumo, where I met most of the characters in this story. The family tree does not contain all of the Bacca descendants but mainly those members referred to in the book to give readers a means to track the relationship of the characters.

The adventures taken throughout this story actually occurred; however, the sequence of events may have been altered to better fit the story. Some of the events took place on my second or third visit to Rumo. In addition, the adventures were not taken with Marcello but with family and friends.

Sadly, Marcello and his family in Torino are the only fictional characters in the story. Therefore, the romance with Marcello is also fictional. I have no doubt that somewhere in Italy is a man named Marcello Dalmasso, yet I have never met him and certainly never fallen in love with him. Nonetheless, I am convinced that if I were ever to meet the man of my dreams, it would have to happen in Rumo, Italy. Why not? Why not!

Acknowledgments

Thank you to my special friend, Debra Bukko, for reading the first draft of this book. She provided me valuable insight that significantly improved the quality of the story. Her enthusiasm and encouragement kept me going through many more revisions.

Thank you also to my family, especially to Jim, Kristina, Kortne, Sarah, and Nadia for their loving support and assistance in editing.

Thank you to the amazing staff and associates at Luminare Press. I could not have published this book without their support, patience, and creativity.

A special thank you to Nadia Lucchini for proofing all things Italian from spelling to historical and family documentation. I am extremely grateful to Nadia and to Caterina Robol for the Italian translation.

www.ingramcontent.com/pod-product-compliance
Lightning Source LLC
LaVergne TN
LVHW012057070526
838200LV00070BA/2783